a girl named Harper

a novel

KARA JEFFERIES

Six Dogs Publications
PO box 407
Prosper, Texas 75078
www.SixDogsPublishing.com
www.karajefferies.com

ISBN 979-8-9896430-4-2 Softcover
ISBN 979-8-9896430-5-9 Digital online

Publisher's Cataloging-In-Publication Data
(Prepared by Cassidy's Cataloguing Services)

Printed in the United States of America

To all the twenty-something
girls out there: embrace change.

Don't be afraid to take risks, pursue your passions,
and rewrite your story as many times as you need.
Your unique voice, talents, and perspective are
needed in the world, and every chapter of your
story is a chance to make a difference.

Prologue

As I reflect on the last twenty-five years of my life, I realize that I am distinctly different from the two individuals who brought me into this world. I have always known this, and yet I have spent my entire life trying to prove to myself that I am not like them.

Last year, I made a promise to myself that I would break the cycle of dysfunction that I grew up in. I vowed to prioritize my own needs, feelings, career, and happiness as a woman. And today, on my twenty-fifth birthday, I can look back and see that I have righted all the wrongs I created, and I am an entirely different person than I was last year.

Some may have said I was mean, but I was really just scared. Some called me cold, but I was simply quiet. Some labeled me as arrogant, yet I was only pretending.

It's raining today, just like it does every year on my birthday. A summer birthday, and it always seems to be accompanied by rain, gloom, and darkness. I used to tell myself that it was a reminder of how much God tests me. But this year, I realize that no matter how gloomy the day is, I will not let external circumstances dictate my happiness. I refuse to let the rain dampen my spirits, and I will celebrate my birthday with the people I love.

Chapter 1

I wake up in my somewhat familiar apartment, and a new scent fills my room. Tobacco mixed with citrus. Not nasty cigarette tobacco but rich tobacco, the kind they use to make candles or men's shampoo. Except I don't have candles or men's shampoo in my apartment. In the haziness of my brain, I replay yesterday in my mind and try to remember how exactly I got into my apartment last night. I do not remember walking up three flights of stairs.

"Hey, you're alive," a smooth baritone voice comes from the chair in my bedroom.

I fall to the floor using my mattress as a giant shield. I push my wild, unbrushed hair from my eyes and peek over the edge of my mattress.

I blurt out, "*What the fuck*! Who are you?"

"I'm your neighbor, well, sort of a neighbor," he says casually as he sinks deeper into my chair. "I saw you moving in this week. Then, last night, I saw you passed out in your car. I stopped to check and make sure you weren't dead. I brought you up here once I realized you wouldn't make it up on your own."

Who is the guy in my apartment with this extremely smooth voice? I feel like a scared child hiding beside my bed, but I do my best to ignore the ridiculous visual and take in all of this man sitting casually on the chair in my bedroom. My eyes travel up his towering frame. He's strong with muscular arms, and one is covered in a tattoo that I can't quite make out. He has olive-tanned skin.

Once my eyes make it to his face, I drink in his dark brown, almost black eyes. Brown eyes are so common, but his are different. His eyes offer no apology for what they may do to you if you stare too long. I have never seen eyes that dark. His face is unshaven, but the scruff can't hide the panty-dropping dimple on his left cheek. Who is this mystery guy with perfectly manicured brown hair, even at this ungodly early hour?

I manage to pull my attention from him before he notices me gawking and ask in quick succession, "What do you mean you just brought me up here? How did you get in? And what does a 'sort of neighbor' mean?"

I'm so full of confusion that I can't think straight. I do not do mornings on a regular day, and today is the furthest thing from ordinary, so to say I'm struggling to grasp what is happening is an understatement at best.

"I used your key," he answers indifferently, like it's a normal occurrence for him to pull sleeping girls from their cars and watch them sleep.

"How did you know what apartment?"

"Like I said, I'm your neighbor." This time, there's a hint of condescension in his voice.

Shit, who is this guy in my apartment? Is he going to kill me?

Just then, as if he were reading my mind, he says, "If I were going to kill you, I would've done it last night when you were passed out in your car."

"Um, I wasn't drunk," I say. "I was…. Never mind, it's none of your business."

My mind wanders back to last night. Why was I asleep in my car? Confusion takes over as some of my fear dissipates, knowing this guy isn't going to kill me in my apartment. I've gotten into some peculiar situations, and this isn't the first time some random guy has been in my home. I was married to a drug addict for a year, so I'm fairly immune to surprises. Maybe that's why I haven't completely lost my mind, or perhaps it's because I'm just super irresponsible.

But who is he? Why did he stay here all night? Why did he even bother helping me? Why didn't he leave me in my car?

"I don't even know your name," I absently say. Then I put my hands in front of my face and blurt out, "I don't want to know your name. Please don't tell me your name. You have to leave!"

As thankful to this guy as I am for what he did for me last night, I can't have him in my apartment any longer. It's weird. It's bizarre.

With that, he gets up to walk out of my bedroom, but before shutting the apartment door and without looking back, I hear him yell, "I'm Gabe, and you're welcome."

Gabe, I repeat to myself.

A hot neighbor named Gabe, whom I've never met, watched me move in last week and last night, sat in my bedroom and watched me sleep. Creepy? Yes. A little heroic? Maybe.

Then, my mind goes to that familiar place of doubt. It's my default setting. Did I snore? Did I grind my teeth? *Shit*, of course I did. I always grind my teeth when I sleep, according to my brother, who shared a wall with me for eighteen years, and Liam, with whom I shared a bed for several years, and with the stress of the last few weeks, there is no doubt in my mind I ground my teeth last night.

How embarring. "*Shit!*" I exclaim, shoving my face into my hands.

Sitting in my bedroom on my floor, I fight the nagging feeling that maybe I overreacted. No average person would feel guilty for kicking some random stranger out of their apartment, regardless of why they ended up there, but that's not me. I feel guilty for everything I say and everything I forget to say. I feel bad for being honest, and I feel bad for lying. I literally can't win over the voices in my head. A dysfunctional childhood takes a toll on one's self-esteem.

There was a strange guy in my apartment when I woke up. Isn't that enough to make any sane person overreact? So why do I feel guilty for kicking him out? Why do I feel guilty for not saying thank you? How does one say, "Thanks for not raping and killing me in my sleep?" Is there a Hallmark card for that?

I fight the urge to crawl back into bed and unravel, but ultimately, I allow myself thirty-nine minutes to feel sorry for myself. Forty minutes felt excessive, and thirty-five minutes wasn't nearly enough time.

I need to figure out what happened last night that required hot neighbor Gabe to rescue me from my car. I'm still sitting on my floor, no longer wielding my mattress as a shield, but leaning against it now. I'm a little more relaxed, with my back and head resting on the side of my bed. I replay last night over in my head. I remember sitting in my car in the parking garage of my new apartment, stewing over how disappointed I was in myself. First, for marrying Liam, whom I had no business even dating, let alone marrying. Second, for not recognizing that my parents were right about him.

I remember being exhausted from moving into my apartment alone because I was too stubborn to ask for help. I remember resting my head on my headrest and getting lost in my thoughts, listening to my favorite song. *Not unlike what I'm doing now.* I remember taking ibuprofen for my sore back and a tinge of a headache.

Just then, it hits me. I trip over my feet as I scramble to my purse, which is untouched and exactly how I left it because not only is Gabe *not* a rapist or murderer, but he's also not a thief either.

I snatch out my two pill containers. One doesn't rattle when I shake it because it's empty. On instinct, I still open it and look inside.

"*Shit*!" I exclaim.

The container that had my sleeping pills is empty, which means I took two sleeping pills, not the two ibuprofen I intended to take.

I quickly scooch over to my nightstand, grab my phone, and hit one of the only two people I have pinned.

"What's wrong?" Julie's voice echoes from my speaker through my bedroom.

"Why does something have to be wrong?" I question.

"You never call, only text, so what happened?" she answers without hesitation.

"Promise not to judge me?" I beg.

"Absolutely not!" she insists.

I have struggled with the fear of judgment my entire life. As a child, my parents had me in modeling; I was never thin enough. As a teenager, they had me in dance; I was never good enough. I didn't invite kids over growing up because our house wasn't in the right zip code, nor did we have the money to belong to the same social clubs as the other kids from school. There has always been a reason I'm not good enough.

"Julie, seriously. You know—"

"For fuck's sake, Harper, I never judge you. Not even when you lied about how you broke your egg baby in fifth grade. Just tell me what happened."

I ponder this confession for a minute. Julie knows all my insecurities, all my lies, and all my fears. Never once in all the years we've been best friends has she ever betrayed me.

"I took too many sleeping pills last night and fell asleep in my car," I blurt.

"On purpose?" she asks, totally confused.

"*No, not on purpose*!" I shout at her. "It gets worse," I add as my tone softens and my speech slows as regret creeps in.

"Harper, I won't judge you. Just tell me what happened. You're beating around the bush like I don't know every one of your darkest secrets and embarrassing moments."

I take a deep, cleansing breath and slowly exhale. "A guy found me in my car and carried me to my apartment. When I woke up, he was still here."

"You're separated from Liam. Who cares," she says, which I take as her permission to move on and not feel guilty about it.

"I didn't sleep with him," I say, shocked that would even come out of her mouth.

"Why not?"

"I fell asleep in my car. He rescued me. Are you even listening to me?" I demand with a huff.

"And you didn't fuck him to thank him?" she asks without shame.

"*Ugh*, No Julie! You're exhausting me," I whine into my phone.

"Okay, so how did you end up in this mess?"

"Well, I remember sitting in my car, feeling unnecessarily sorry for myself and being pissed off at my parents—"

"Nothing out of the ordinary there."

She's not wrong. I can go from being pissed off to feeling sorry for myself to feeling guilty in under a second when it comes to my parents.

"Do you think I'll ever not be so hot and cold when it comes to my parents?" I ask.

"Probably not," she answers. "It's all you have from your childhood. Separate, your parents are great. Together, they're toxic."

I am twenty-four years old and still carry emotional baggage from my childhood. Seeing my mom forgive my dad's affairs and excuse his abuse has made it difficult for me to trust men or fall in love with them.

Julie continues, "Do you remember when your dad showed up to cheer practice with his arm bandaged?

"How can I forget?" I reply.

"He got drunk and beat the shit out of your mom and brother the night before. You felt guilty. It wasn't you. You felt sorry for him because he was alone. You kept saying, 'Why did he never hit me?' Harper, that's not normal."

"I think it is normal, Dr. Julie. It's called survivor guilt. They literally have a label for it."

She sighs. "See, you always find a reason to justify your crazy thoughts."

My dad never once laid a hand on me, even if I deserved it. Trust me, there were plenty of times when I gave him reason to.

"Why do you think he never hit me?" I ask.

"Because he loved you more."

"Julie, seriously!" I argue.

"I am being serious. You just don't want to hear that no matter how fucked up your parents were to each other, they both still loved you more than anything."

Pondering that statement, I remembered when I had to stay with family and friends. My mom had once again lost her mind, and they were separating. They agreed they didn't want to put me in the middle. Although they never stayed apart for more than a week or two, it was challenging for me to pivot from *the sky falling* to *your dad will be home tonight.*

The line is quiet for a minute, and Julie asks, "How are you dealing with being apart from Liam?"

"Fine, I guess," I say. "Being apart from Liam isn't my problem. A failed marriage is a huge problem for me. Seeing everyone at the holidays without him and having to explain what went wrong. Then there's his family. What are they saying about me? Or, worse, our shared friends. Which, by the way, no one has reached out to me since we separated."

"They weren't your friends. They were his, and they just tolerated you." I cringe when she says this. "His family will talk about you whether you're good or bad, and you still have the few people who matter, so stop caring so much about what everyone thinks about you." Her tone is softer now.

The ups and downs of being raised in a dysfunctional family helped me see pretty early on that my marriage to Liam was never going to work. We were married for only a year, but we lived together for almost four years on and off. I met Liam during my junior year of high school. He was five years older than me and would be my ticket to freedom. He had a great family and a bright future in his family's business, but ultimately, I realized he would never be the one for me.

Julie breaks my thought and continues, "You didn't give up too quickly." Again, trying to reassure me

"Maybe not," I say somberly.

"And, seriously, Harper, what if they're right? What if you ended your marriage too early? Too early for who? There is a fine line between being too early and waiting too long to leave. They will judge you no matter what, so please, for the love of all things good, stop caring so much about what everyone thinks about you," Julie continues her rant. "This has always been your issue. You grew up in a toxic house raised by drug addicts. You have kept secrets your entire life to save yourself from judgment. At some point, you will have to accept that you may not be for everyone, and you need to love yourself regardless of others' expectations. You are a flawed human, Harper Atwood. Embrace it!"

I laugh into the phone and say, "Technically, I'm jobless since I don't start my new job until next week. I'm twenty-four and almost divorced, even though it was by my doing, and you're telling me to embrace that mess?"

"Loud and proud!" she answers. "Listen, I have to run. Stop beating yourself up because you're not the CEO of a company and married to the perfect guy with two dogs and two kids. You'll get to where you're supposed to be eventually. Stop reading self-help books and read some smut. You won't feel so bad about your failed marriage or the fact some random man was in your apartment last night, but you didn't fuck him. If you're worried about being judged, that's the one thing I'm judging you for."

"I can't decide if I hate or love you more."

"Love, it's definitely love," she jokes. "Oh, if you see Xavier, tell him I still want his body.

"That's my cousin, and he's off limits to you. We've been over this."

She hangs up without saying bye, but that's not out of the ordinary for her. She says she's not one for goodbyes.

Chapter 2

I look around my apartment, which is almost free of moving boxes and trash bags, and can't help but feel the tiniest bit of pride. I've accomplished the thing I should've done at eighteen... Independence. I start my new job next week. I have a new place. I think I can do this single-boss babe thing everyone talks about.

Looking in the mirror, I tilt my head back and forth, pop one leg in front of the other, put my hands on my hips, and say aloud, "Look at you. All grown up, living alone and supporting yourself. Welcome to your boss babe era, Harper Atwood."

But this independent, all-grown-up girl is starving, and I have no food in my apartment. So, I do what all independent women do...I call my mom. Her face appears on my phone.

"I can't survive on coffee alone. Are you hungry?" I ask.

"Always," she cheerfully answers.

"Let's meet at our spot," I say.

We don't have any traditions in my family. No family dinners on Thursday or Sunday fun days. But my mom and I make it a point to meet at our favorite deli as often as possible.

We don't spend much time together, so lunch a few times a month is good for my soul. As much as I blame my mom (and dad) for my dysfunctional childhood, I understand that no one is ever really prepared to raise kids, especially when you're barely old enough to take care of yourself.

I love my mom a lot. I also blame my mom for a lot. I've always feared being judged (by everyone), so I didn't allow myself to have any close friends aside from Julie. This pushed me to confide in my mom maybe a little too much, which opened up the opportunity for my mom to over-share with me. My mom would share bits and pieces about her childhood, probably more than most mothers would, trying to justify why she stayed with my dad. But her doing so helped me understand who my mom is and why.

Mom and I meet at our deli. It's within walking distance of my apartment, which is a remarkable coincidence. I see Mom sitting at our table, and I wave.

"Hey babe," my mom says with a smile.

She grazes my hand. I *hate* physical touch. It makes me uncomfortable, and I'm very awkward at it.

My mom has constantly smothered me with touch. She used to try to hold my hand in public when I was in high school. No fifteen-year-old wants to hold their mom's hand in public, but then I'd feel guilty for telling her no because all my mom wanted was to feel close to me.

My mom is pretty. She always has been. She's five foot three inches, much shorter than me at five foot eleven inches. She has long dark hair that she highlights often. I have bright blonde hair. But we both share her green eyes. Her eyes tell a different story than mine, though. Her eyes hide secrets of abuse.

Mom ended up pregnant with my brother at seventeen. She and my dad got married in his mom's backyard when my mom was eight months pregnant.

Waiting for our food, my mom asks, "How is your new apartment?"

"It's nice. I'm almost all unpacked and boxes cleaned up." I sit up a little taller when I answer.

"Wow, were your dad and brother able to help?"

"No, Brandon couldn't get off work, and Dad was busy."

With furrowed brows and a wrinkled forehead, she asks, "So, who helped you?"

"No one," I answer. "I moved what I could by myself and left what I couldn't."

"Furniture?" she questions, not trying to hide her judgment directed solely at my dad.

"Hired a company for the big stuff. Dad couldn't help me lift all that anyway. It was just a ton of boxes and clothes."

She crosses her arms and questions, "He was busy?"

I don't answer her question because it was never intended to be a question but a judgment.

I sit back in my chair and ask, "Why did you stay with Dad as long as you did?"

I always thought my mom stayed with my dad despite all his lies and deception because she had low self-esteem, and maybe that is part of it, but I feel like I owe it to her to hear her "why," especially since I left my husband after only a year of marriage.

"Harper, I was forced from a young age to fight to keep myself safe. I didn't have anyone to protect me. I knew what happened when a man raised someone else's child. I didn't want that for you or your brother. I knew your dad cheated often. I've never denied that to you. Maybe I shared too many details with you in retrospect."

She pauses for a minute, and I can see her brain bouncing back and forth from her childhood to her marriage to my dad and her present day. Her green eyes look sad. Like they have hidden more hurt than she'll ever admit to me.

She continues, "I chose not to leave. I chose ignorance, not for me, but for you and your brother. If I left your father, I'd have no control over what happened to you and your brother in his house. I ensured I was there every day after school. I got to sing to you on your birthday, and I chose that there would be no separate holidays. You see, Harper, I was willing to sacrifice having only half a husband to have a hundred percent of you and your brother."

Needing to satisfy the burning question I've had my entire childhood but was always too afraid to ask, I ask, "Why did you let him hit you?"

"It was only a few times," she answers as she looks away from avoiding eye contact.

I roll my eyes. "You're making excuses for him, Mom. One time is too many."

"I was abused my entire childhood, Harper. I didn't know any better. Your dad's few drunken indiscretions were nothing compared to what my father did to me."

She looks down at the table and arranges her silverware as if a memory returned to her, and it hurts too bad to look at me. I think she stopped loving her dad long before he passed several years ago. And whatever she feels for him today is solely out of obligation.

Then my mom looks up and asks, "Why did you leave Liam so quickly?"

Shaking my head, I answer as honestly as I can, "I knew it was never going to work. He is a drug addict, and I want something different than my childhood. I wasn't going to change him. I don't want that life for me anymore."

Putting her hand on mine to emphasize her point, she says,

"I'm glad you left when you did." Her statement has no malice. There's no, *I told you so*—just pure relief and approval.

"I know you are," I say quietly.

It's nice to spend time with my mom, and it's helpful for me to have these conversations with her. "Mom, I know you feel guilty and think I need a do-over childhood, but it's impossible not to love you." I continue, "Now that you and Dad are no longer together, you can forgive yourself for whatever you're holding on to. I don't want a do-over, and I don't want a better mom next time. My childhood made me who I am."

"Harper, you'll make an amazing mom," she says, rubbing my hand.

Inventively, I rip my hand from under hers and hold them both up in surrender.

"I don't want kids. I've never wanted kids," I whisper-shout at her. "Mom, I can't keep another human alive. This meal right here may be the only thing I eat today. Forgetting to feed myself is one thing. Forgetting to feed a child is a criminal offense."

She laughs.

There is something very overwhelming about wanting to put someone's needs before yours. Remember, I'm the girl who just took two sleeping pills instead of an ibuprofen.

I continued to whisper-yell at her, needing to get my point across, "Mom, unconditional love isn't a concept I understand. I don't think it would be fair for me to mother a child. Even if I managed to keep it alive, I'm not sure I could love it enough."

"Never short of dramatics, Harper, are you?" she jokes. Then she changes the subject completely and asks, "Tell me about your new job. Have you started yet?"

"No, next week. I still need to do pre-employment paperwork," I continue.

"Are you at least excited?"

I shrug and say, "It's a job, mom, not a vacation. I'm excited to get my life back on track, if that's what you're asking."

"Maybe you'll make a few friends there. Take some pressure off Julie."

Immediately, I feel the weight of her judgment. I try my best not to ruin our lunch by blowing up on her, so I calmly say, "Mom, being a friend to me is not a chore that Julie needs a reprieve from."

She huffs. "Harper, don't be dramatic. I didn't mean it like that. I meant it would be nice to meet new people with whom you can interact casually now that you're an adult."

"I'm the boss, Mom. Hanging out with people and telling them what to do and when doesn't translate well outside of work. Can we put the whole 'Harper, you need to make more friends' debate to sleep? We've been having this argument my entire life."

Mom crosses her arms. "Have you talked to your uncle since he helped you get the job?"

"Not really. And, Mom, he didn't help me get the job. He just recommended me for the job. I was able to get the job based on my reputation. At some point, you'll have to stop giving your brother all the credit for my career."

She sighs as if I'm being dramatic, but I'm not. He recommended me for a job. I interviewed with five different executives. Eventually, my parents will have to see I'm an adult and I'm actually good at what I do.

"What will you be doing for the dealership, Harper?" she asks.

"I will be the sales manager for their E-commerce department. It's a new department, so I don't think anyone knows exactly what I'll be doing, but the money is good, and being newly single, that's all that matters to me right now. I'm so thankful to have the opportunity to care for myself for once."

I take the last bite of my sandwich, not knowing when I'll have time to get to the store and have food in my apartment.

"Do you need a back-to-work outfit?" she asks, knowing I'll never refuse a new outfit.

"Mom, I need therapy, not retail therapy! But you know I'll never refuse a new back-to-work outfit if you're buying."

She laughs. No one knows me like my mom knows me.

Chapter 3

GABE

I arrive at Joy's house early, so we have enough time to stop for coffee before we arrive at the airport. I push the up button on the elevator, and without delay, the doors open. I hit the button for the third floor, and I can't help but replay the other night in my head. Joy lives in the same apartment building where I found a girl passed out in her car. I took Joy's car to work that day to get it serviced. I'm a sales manager for a Toyota dealership. Taking care of Joy's car is something I enjoy doing for her, even though she works at a different dealership across town.

I was parking her car in her designated spot when I saw her new neighbor. I noticed her moving in last week but didn't pay her any attention until that night when I took her to her apartment. She's thin and tall, all legs. I know this because they draped over my arms while carrying her to her apartment like a baby.

When she woke up and freaked out the next day, I can't say I got a much better view of her since she hid behind her bed the entire time. It was cute. She reminded me of a scared child. I guess I can't blame her. I had so many questions, and she offered me zero opportunity to ask her anything. I didn't even get her name. I didn't even get a thank you. It's weird, though I can't stop thinking about her. I never obsess over girls, especially ones who have a ton of issues. And this girl was passed out in her car. We all know she must have a long list of issues.

Stepping off the elevator at Joy's floor makes it impossible for me not to focus down a few doors, hoping the girl who has been living in my head walks out of her apartment and recognizes me. Just then, Joy swings her door open, snapping me back to reality.

"Good morning," she sings.

And I expect nothing less from her. Joy is short and has a petite frame. Her champaign-colored hair sits just below her shoulders, and she has dark, deep blue eyes like the ocean and a small smattering of freckles across the bridge of her nose.

"Ready to go?" I ask, trying either to get into her apartment or the elevator. Anywhere but in the middle of the hallway that she shares with my mystery girl.

"Ready!" she exclaims, all smiles. "I can't believe it's been a month since my birthday," she adds, giddy like a kid on Christmas.

"You know I would've preferred to take you on this surprise birthday trip on your actual birthday last month, right?"

"Yes, I know, but our schedules wouldn't allow it," she says as she shrugs off my concern. Joy never complains. She's never emotional. She's perfect.

Joy and I have been dating off and on for six months. We're not serious or exclusive. We have a great time together and great sex. We are both on the same page as far as our relationship is concerned. We're two adults hanging out and having a good time until one of us moves on.

We also agreed to remain friends once things end. If that stays accurate, great. If not, I'm also okay with that. Joy is a fantastic human, always full of positivity. It's as if her parents knew who she'd become when they named her Joy. It's impossible to be in a bad mood when she is around.

I open Joy's car door for her and load her suitcase into the trunk of my car.

She yells back at me, "I'm so excited for this weekend. I've been dying with excitement. Are you as excited as I am?"

I hesitate for a minute as I think about how selfish I am. Joy has been looking forward to this trip for far too long for me to ruin it by constantly thinking of a mystery girl with no name that I can't seem to get out of my head.

"Umm yeah, I can't wait to get away for a few days with you," I reply.

Once we're comfortable in our seats on the plane, I ask Joy, "Have you seen your new neighbor? You know the one I told you about?"

I told Joy about the girl I found in her garage and why I never came to her apartment that night. But I didn't tell her the truth about how this girl has been consuming my mind for unknown reasons.

Totally oblivious to the motivation behind my question, she replies, "No, not at all."

A little relieved they haven't met, I sink back in my seat. I have to stop thinking about her. This weekend is about Joy, not me.

The plane ride is short. Once we get to the resort and settle into our room, I ask, "What's first?"

With a perplexed look on her face, she says, "The slopes," as if no other options exist.

"Snowboarding it is, then," I agree, take her hand, and usher her to the slopes.

Once on the ski lift, she leans in and nudges against me. "You okay? You look like you have a lot on your mind."

If I were honest with Joy about what was happening in my head, she would take time and calm my racing mind without judgment. She would talk through it with me and probably give me the advice I desperately need, but this trip isn't about me. It's about her.

Trying not to lie, I turn my attention to the snow-capped mountains and answer, "No, I'm good. I can't stop thinking about the girl I helped at your apartment the other day. It's bizarre that I found her sleeping in their car downstairs from her apartment."

"She told you she was fine the following day when you scared the shit out of her by watching her sleep, right?" she jokes.

I shove her with my body as we work our way up the mountain and say, "Stop! I'm not a creeper. I'm a concerned neighbor. I would've felt so bad if something happened to her." I rub my hand over my face and add, "I have no idea why I always get myself mixed up in other people's issues."

Five hours on a snowboard is way too long for me. "I'm too old for this, Joy," I groan as I rub my ass and down my hamstrings.

She gives me a sweet smile and laughs. "Let's go in and get ready for dinner, old man."

I shake my head and lead us to the lodge. Once inside, it's warm. I feel my frozen hands tingle, and they come back to life. Joy leads us to our room, and with the day's soreness continuing to set in and take over my entire body, I struggle to keep up.

Joy, a little more playful than usual, looks back and shouts back as she maintains her ten-step lead. "Do you need a ride on my back, old man?"

"Stop, Joy, or you're eating alone tonight," I joke.

The multiple shower heads do wonders on all my sore muscles.

Joy shouts from the bathroom as she prepares for dinner, "Don't lay down, Gabe. If you do, you'll never get up."

I shout back, "Joy, just because I feel like an eighty-year-old man doesn't mean I am one. Seriously, I can stay up for dinner."

Rolling over, I'm awakened by the sun's brightness reflecting off the snow. "Awhhhh, shit!" I moan as I rub sleep from my eyes.

Joy rolls toward me and whispers in a sleepy voice, "I told you not to lay down, old man."

"Shit, Joy, I'm sorry I ruined dinner for you last night."

"Gabe, you didn't ruin anything for me. I came out of the bathroom. You looked so comfortable that I grabbed my book, changed into jammies, and crawled beside you in bed. I couldn't dream of a better night.

"Eating," I argue. "Eating would have made your night better."

"Who said I didn't eat? I called down and got wine and a sandwich sent up. You know I don't need fancy dinners, Gabe."

The drive back home from the airport is quiet, so I allow music to fill the conversation void, which has never been an issue for Joy and me. My phone rings, and I quickly answer it. Again, this is something other than what I would typically do with Joy in the car.

"Hey Mark," I answer the phone more chipper than usual.

"Hey, Gabe, I have a favor to ask. We have a new hire coming in tomorrow for a management position, and I need you to help navigate the new hire process. Can you come in an hour earlier to help?"

"Sure," I answer, all too happily volunteer.

This is so not like me. I don't mind doing favors for the guys, but coming in early from a long weekend isn't one of them since we always stay late to close deals.

I ask Mark, "Is it a new hire for our dealership?"

I'm hoping to prolong the conversation to fill the awkward silence in the car.

"No, I think she'll be at a different dealership," Mark answers matter-of-factly.

"Oh good," I say, relieved. "The last thing we need is another manager on the desk. We could actually lose one or two and be better off than we are now."

"Agreed," he replies.

"See you tomorrow."

Then I hang up.

"Look at you, you're going in early," Joy teases. "You better be careful, or you'll end up like me."

Joy is a sales manager at another dealership, a competitor of ours. She works all the time. She goes in early and stays late. She takes weekend shifts for the married guys. All she asks for in return is a coffee or lunch. I always tell her to stop and that the guys will take advantage of her charity, but she doesn't listen. Her best friend Roxanne works in the business office. Outside of Roxy and me, Joy doesn't hang out or even go out. She says she doesn't mind, and it makes her feel good to help when she can. That's just the type of person she is. She's perfect, but is she perfect for me?

I feel refreshed the next morning, driving into work to help with the new hire. It's amazing what a few days off can do to help reset your mindset. Walking in from the side entrance, rarely used by customers, I say hello to everyone in the Internet department working away at their computers. I have always tried to say hello to everyone individually, always making eye contact and taking the time to fist-bump everyone. The Internet department doesn't report to me, but I don't want them to feel like I think any less of their contributions to the company.

I approach the sales desk with one of the guys, Landon. I

casually tell him about my ski trip. I feel a strange surge of butterflies in my stomach, almost like static electricity has taken over our entire dealership. The feeling pulls my attention from Landon straight to the reception desk.

It's the girl from Joy's apartment garage. The girl I carried to her apartment and stayed with to ensure she was okay, only for her to freak out and kick me out in the morning without a thank you or explanation. She technically didn't owe me an explanation for why she was passed out in her car or a thank you, but either would've been nice.

I hear Landon say my name. "Hey Gabe, you okay?"

I look at him, a little surprised, and say, "Oh, sorry, I was distracted. What did you ask me?"

I'm still staring at my mystery girl from the garage, just standing there talking to our receptionist. Both of them are totally oblivious to me.

She has on tight pants and a black low-cut top that's tucked in. She is thin and small-chested, but her tits are perfect. She has to be almost six feet tall without heels, so she's probably over six feet when she wears them.

He asks me again, "What resort did you stay at? I'm looking to head up next week. I have two consecutive days off."

"Oh, it's called Snowed Inn Lodge," I answer quickly. "Hey, I have to run. I think the girl at the reception desk is here for me."

I don't think that is a true statement. I have no idea why she is here. Did she figure out who I am and come to thank me? Is she buying a car, and is this a coincidence? Whatever it is, the universe put her in my workplace, and I intend to find out her name and how she found out where I work.

Landon looks in that direction, smiles, and says, "Always the charmer, Gabe. Good luck, but this one may be out of your league."

I watch her as I make my way to the reception desk. Mark is already there with her. She politely smiles as Mark introduces himself. She's put together and confident but still reserved. This is a very different side of the girl who kicked me out of her apartment last week. That girl was confused and out of control.

I watch her as she reaches out to shake Mark's hand, and a weird jolt of possessiveness takes over my body.

As I slowly approach them, Mark sees me and shouts, "Gabe! Come on over and meet Harper. Harper, this is Gabe, the sales manager I was telling you about. He'll walk you through your new hire paperwork and show you around the dealership."

Totally caught off guard, I look between Mark and the mystery girl.

"Gabe," Mark says in a low voice. "You okay?"

Without hesitation, the mystery girl reaches out her hand and grabs mine. "Nice to meet you, Gabe. I'm Harper Atwood."

She takes my hand and shakes it. I hold on to her for a few seconds too long and find myself completely lost in her green eyes.

She releases my hand, and I stammer breathlessly over my next words, "N...Nice to meet you, Harper."

In her apartment that morning, she had just woken up, her hair was messy, and she stayed hidden behind her mattress the whole time, so I never saw her body, let alone her eyes. They're green like a four-leaf clover in spring. I knew she was tall and thin because I carried her up three stories. But she is like nothing I've ever seen. She's breathtaking, and I have a feeling she has no idea what she does when she walks into a room. Her presence demands attention; she owns the room. The girl here is confident. I find myself standing up straighter and talking a little louder than usual to keep her attention on me.

She finally speaks again, "Are you okay, Gabe? You look like you've seen a ghost."

Shaking my head and trying to hide my embarrassment, I lie, "Yeah, I'm fine." *I am not fine,* I think to myself. "You just look so familiar," I manage to say.

Does she not recognize me? I have to ask her, but I don't want to have this conversation in front of Mark. It might embarrass her, so I'm trying to play it cool but failing miserably. I need to get her alone.

Mark looks between us and says, "Harper, he's not acting like it, but you are in excellent hands. Gabe will handle your paperwork and answer any questions you have." As Mark walks away, he whispers, "Pull yourself together, man. You're embarrassing yourself. You're acting like a seventh-grade school boy with a crush."

I hear Harper snort under her breath, and I can't hide my embarrassment for apparent reasons, but I am equally frustrated that Harper has no idea who I am.

As Mark walks away, the realization of being alone with her hits me, and my stomach starts to flip as if it's competing in the summer Olympics and about to win a gold medal on the uneven bars. I want to demand an explanation about that night from her but remind myself this isn't the time or the place.

Not knowing what to say or do next is unlike me. I'm the life of the party. I'm the loud one who dances in sales meetings and doesn't care what people say about me. But at this moment, I don't know what to say or how to act. The spell that she has over me is totally foreign.

"Do you know what you'll be doing at the dealership?" I ask.

Of course, she knows what job she applied for. What a stupid question, Gabe. Come on...get it together.

Confused, she asks with a tilt of her head, "Like, do I know what I'm going to be doing next week when I start working? Of course I do. I'm going to run the Internet sales department or the E-commerce sales department.

Confused, I ask, "Well, which one?"

"Which one what?" she asks.

This interaction is going terribly.

"Which department? Internet or E-commerce?"

She laughs, puts her hand on my shoulder, and says, "So... You're the resident jokester, I see."

I tilt my head and look at her, confused.

She quickly adds, "Oh, you're serious." Again, she's trying not to laugh at my expense and continues, "Well, the Internet and E-commerce departments are the same thing. Some call it the Internet department, and others call it the E-commerce department."

Feeling like an idiot, I nod, and she gives me a pitying sigh.

"Would you believe me if I told you I knew that and was just testing you?" I ask.

"Nope, not a chance," she retorts, not even offering a look in my direction.

Curious, I ask, "How did you get the job for the auto group. I don't recall us placing an ad for an E-commerce manager. I'm curious."

She asks if I want the extended version or the Cliffs notes, and since I'm trying to drag out our time together as long as possible, we all know my answer.

"Long version, I guess," I answer her.

"This position was created for me based on a recommenda-tion from my uncle. He has a hand in everything and knows everyone. I'm good at what I do, actually very good at what I do. I sell shit, teach people to sell shit, and motivate the hell out of my teams. I motivate them to want to work for me. I help them make more money than they would without me. I thrive at work. I'm the best version of myself at work. I'm comfortable and in control."

I stare at her, not knowing what to say next, so she continues, "The auto group must expand its E-commerce presence. Online car shopping is taking off and quickly becoming the preferred method to start the car buying process. It shows no signs of slowing down, especially with the continuing increase in Internet shopping and the simple fact that people hate the car-buying process. Car salesmen have a terrible reputation, rightfully so, for being dishonest."

"Hey...Hey," I interrupt her. "You're starting to sound like an anti-car buying commercial. We're on the same team here," I add.

"Seriously, Gabe, are you going to disagree?"

"While car salesmen may have a bad reputation, we have a lot of good people here who are trying to do right by our customers."

The worst part of my job is trying to overcome the stereotype that follows car salesmen.

"Fine," she continues. "Moving forward, my department will completely change how people buy cars. People will have quotes in hand, giving them the power back and cutting down the time it takes to buy a vehicle in person. The need for someone to manage the Internet sales team is undeniable. I am now that person." Without taking a breath, she asks, "Where to go next?"

My head is spinning. I'm trying to digest everything she just said and how it'll inevitably affect the sales team at the dealership where she lands. There will be tension between her team and the sales team. Is she aware of what exactly she is walking into? She's so confident I assume that she's not going into this blindly. I'm just glad she won't be here.

"I'll take you to the business office, and you can do your paperwork there."

"Sounds good," she says.

After completing her mountain of paperwork, I give her a tour around the dealership for no other reason than to spend as much time with her as possible. After today, I'll only see her when I visit Joy, which is awkward, and at company Christmas parties. Christmas is the only time the entire auto group gets together, but the odds of us seeing each other are slim.

I know she won't be working here, so I have to make the most of our time today. Walking her through the showroom, I can feel all eyes on us. Maybe not us, but definitely on her. The receptionists are younger girls, generally in their late teens and early twenties, and the judgment on their faces could be felt from a mile away. It's hard not to smirk. The receptionists are used to getting all the sales guys' attention, and watching them spiral is entertaining.

"Well, that looks like the end of our tour," I say, debating if I should say something now to her about who I am.

"It was nice to meet you, Gabe. I appreciate you spending a few hours with me today. I know it sucks to draw the short straw and have to babysit the new girl."

Before I can say anything else, she is already walking away. She looks over her shoulder and says, "Thanks again. I'll see you soon."

And I can't help but wonder what she means by that. How will she see me soon? Did she recognize me and think she'd see me at the apartment? Panic sets in when I realize I wasn't fully honest with her that morning. Does she think *I* live there, not my girlfriend?

"Dammit," I mutter under my breath as I shove my hand

through my hair. I knew I should've said something when I had the chance.

Today has been the longest day of my career. I spent three hours with Harper first thing this morning, and the rest of the day has been dragging. I skipped lunch so I could leave an hour or so early, but now not only am I distracted by Harper, but I'm also starving. I can't stop thinking about her. I can't stop thinking about her perfume's sweet, subtle scent and her not-so-subtle green eyes.

The vibration of my phone snaps me out of my trance, and I am pleased to see the name and picture that light up my phone.

"Hey sunshine, I've been waiting for your call all day."

"Oh, have you," Joy says. "I've been waiting for you to come to my place and fuck me all day, so I guess we're even."

"I'll be off in an hour or so, and I'll be at your place."

My mind is still racing as I drive to Joy's apartment. I can't believe the mystery girl finally has a name, and I know where she works. I don't know exactly which dealership she works at, but at least I can find her.

• • •

"Earth to Gabe...Hello...Are you here?"

"Oh yeah, sorry. Long day at work, and I have a lot on my mind," I continue, "Joy, there's a girl. I've barely spoken to her, but I don't feel right doing this." I gesture between us and continue, "While thinking about her."

"Gabe, I don't care that you met a girl."

"I know you don't, Joy. But I feel guilty, and I can't lead you on," I say, pleading with her to understand and not make this any harder for me than it is.

"Friends?" she asks as she sticks out her hand.

"Friends," I parrot as an overwhelming sense of relief floods over me.

Chapter 4

Three hours into my first day at work, I still haven't seen Gabe, and I hate myself for obsessing about it. Whenever the receptionist welcomes someone as they walk in, I look up to see if it's him. When he walked up and shook my hand during my orientation, I thought I would have a heart attack in the middle of the dealership.

First, what are the odds that the one person who has seen me at my worst actually works at my new job? Not to mention that he will most likely resent me because our teams will be competing. Lastly, did he even recognize me? He had at least five opportunities to question me about that night in my apartment, but nothing came of it. He has to know I'm the girl. How could he not know?

Just then, the side door flies open, filling the air with a familiar scent of tobacco and citrus.

God, I love that smell.

There he is, all six feet tall of him. Gabe is wearing a button-down black dress shirt, but his sleeves are rolled up to his elbows, showing off the tattoo on his right arm. It was covered the last time I was here, but I remember it from that morning in my apartment. His arms are muscular, and his shirt does nothing to hide it.

"Shit," I whisper to myself as I slide down in my chair so my head isn't visible above my cubical wall.

I remain slumped down, barely breathing until I can devise a plan of what to do next.

After a minute or so, I can't think of a plan (I've never had an issue being an on-the-fly type of girl, but he's throwing me off my game). Needing to see what's happening, I slowly ease up enough for him to see me, but I pretend to be busy. Everybody seems to love him.

He walks up to everyone's desk and hands out fist bumps as if he just walked off the sports field after taking his team to the championship game. He acknowledges everyone but me. I know he saw me. He couldn't miss me. He had to have seen me. He knew someone was sitting here even if he didn't recognize it was me. *What a dick.* Why didn't he say hello to me? I think I hate this man already.

All the sales managers sit in an elevated office together that is high enough that they can get an unobstructed view of the entire sales floor. I opted to sit with my team to engage with them, help them, and really make a difference. It's not common for people to have lengthy careers at dealerships, which is why I feel compelled to make the most of this opportunity by sharing my sales knowledge to grow my team. Nor do I want to spend eight hours daily in a twelve-foot-long shoebox office with four to eight men.

Not sitting with the sales managers only means I have to walk back and forth to interact with them, which is inevitable when creating a new company division. I've already been in there four times in the last three hours. I've been leaning on Mark for help until I can get my arms around everything. He's an older man in his early fifties. He's overweight, and you can tell sales have taken their toll on him. He's one of California's last smokers and a very proud holdout.

Reluctantly, I walk into their office for the fifth time today. I'm not reluctant about asking so many questions. I'm reluctant because Gabe is there now, and he adds another layer of something I can't quite describe. I was excited to see him an hour ago, but after he ignored me, I don't think I ever want to see him again.

Walking in, I completely avoid eye contact with Gabe, but I can feel his stare burning a hole into my back. Still ignoring him, I ask Mark a slew of questions I have written down because I knew I would lose my train of thought once I got in there.

As I speak to Mark, he must notice some confusion on Gabe's face because he asks, "Gabe, you remember Harper, right?"

"Umm, yeah, but I didn't realize she was working here with us."

Gabe stumbles over his words, and I can't help but smirk. What is he so confused about?

Surprised, I look at Mark and shrug. I ask Gabe directly, "Where else would I work? This is the corporate office."

Gabe and Mark exchange a look that I can't make out. Mark looks apologetic, and Gabe looks irritated.

"What am I missing?" I ask, not wanting to play guessing games.

Mark again looks to Gabe as if he's asking for permission, but Gabe answers before Mark can. "When you came in for your pre-hire paperwork, I was under the impression it was for a different dealership."

"Makes sense," I say, annoyed. "Not sure why it matters to you where I work."

I turn to quickly walk away.

"Harper," he calls my name as I walk out of the office, and I can feel it in my chest. "Well, for what it's worth, I'm glad you're here."

"Gabe," I call back, and he lifts his head to look me straight in the eyes, and I say. "Then maybe tomorrow, when you walk in and fist-bump my team, you can also say hello to me."

"I promise I didn't see you." He shouts.

I tilt my head, raise one eyebrow, and shrug at him as I turn away for the second time.

I hear the other managers giving him a hard time as I return to my desk. I can't help but obsess over the things I didn't say that I wanted to say or the things I did say that didn't need to be said. That is my toxic trait. I can't help my mind from wandering down that terrible path. Then I remind myself I desperately need therapy.

Chapter 5

GABE

When she leaves the manager's office, I feel all mixed up in my emotions. I'm frustrated that she didn't say she'd be working here with me. I'm mad at myself for not asking her what dealership she'd be working at. How stupid am I for not asking?

Then, I'm ecstatic that we are working together but frustrated that I'm happy we're working together. I'm confused about why she still hasn't said anything about the first night. She has to know I'm the guy. Why is she not acknowledging me? And, I'm furious at her for living in my head for the past few weeks, and now knowing I'll never get away from her.

I rub my hand over my face, and Mark asks, "You okay, man?"

Shaking my head, I try to divert my frustration from Harper to something that won't make me look insane. "No, I'm not okay! Why did no one tell me we were hiring another manager? You all understand we get bonuses based on sales that we divide between us managers. Now, she's," I say, waving my hand toward her desk. "Just one more person that gets a cut." Feeling the gravity of what is happening around me, I say,

"Wait, stop. What just happened? Mark, I asked you if the new hire was working here, and you said no. What changed?"

Mark shrugs. "First off, stop with the temper tantrum, Gabe. It's not the end of the world. She was brought here from the top. She's the family of someone." He's waving his hand around as if none of this is important to anyone but me. "They don't ask permission. They just make decisions, and at the last minute, she got moved to the corporate office."

"Who is she related to?" I ask.

She mentioned her uncle knows someone, but does her uncle work for us? This girl is becoming more and more mysterious.

"I don't know," Mark says, clearly over all my questions. "But I also heard she's good at leading a team, so maybe you can give her a chance."

"Who said I wasn't," I say, a little offended. I put my hand over my heart for dramatics.

Mark rolls his eyes. "Gabe, seriously, we have the largest E-commerce sales department for the auto group, so it makes sense for her to be here."

"What exactly is her job?" I ask, annoyed that Mark isn't wrong.

He continues, "She's going to grow and manage the E-commerce sales team. I do know she runs her show here. She has the hours she wants. She works in the office she wants. Damn, I wouldn't be surprised if they let her fire and hire whom she wants. Sorry, man, it's not personal. You can interact with her as much or as little as you choose, but remember, she reports back to the top. Her boss is far above any of us."

I nod my head in understanding and say, "Yeah, she said something similar the day she signed her paperwork. I just never thought she'd end up here."

Landon, one of the sales managers that Mark introduced her to the first day she came to the office, chimes in and adds,

"She's quiet. If you aren't interacting directly with her, you'd never know she was here. She keeps to herself. What's your malfunction, Gabe? I thought you two got along the other day?"

"I need to walk," I say and rush out the front door so I don't have to walk past her on the way out. I can hear the guys behind me as I walk out, asking why I'm so pissed.

I push my hands through my hair and say, "Is this happening? This girl, who finally has a name and has been unknowingly consuming my headspace, works with me. I'm never going to get her out of my mind now."

The Grind is a block away, not far enough to calm my racing mind. The guys think I'm just upset because Harper was hired. I'm a little pissed we have another manager, but couldn't it be anyone else? There are eight billion people on this earth, and Harper is the person we hired to run our E-commerce department. Just my shit luck.

I know I look like an asshole to all the other managers, but I couldn't care less about the office politics that surround why and how she got here. I'm pissed because I see her green eyes everywhere I look. I smell her sweet perfume when she plays the main character in my fantasies. In the shower stroking my dick, she is the one I see. It's her, no one else. I spent three days in the mountains with Joy and only thought about Harper.

The guilt over how much I thought about her during Joy's birthday weekend trip, when I should've been focused on Joy, hits me. I notice sweat building on my brow despite it being a chilly September day.

I've been a playboy in the past and not overly cared about women and their emotions, but I've tried the last few years to change who I am, and Joy helped me see the person I could be. I didn't want to hurt her.

Chapter 6

"You can't avoid me forever, Harper Atwood," sings a familiar voice. I look over my shoulder to see my cousin Xavier standing across the hall.

"Yes, I can," I sing back with a bit too much excitement. "Who sent you here, Xavier?" I ask as I unlock my apartment door.

Following me in, he says, "My mom and your dad. Your dad is worried about you. He's left you a few messages, and, in his words, you're either dead or ignoring him. So, my mom called and asked me to check on you."

Xavier and I are close. Much closer now that we're adults. He's four years older than me and belongs to my dad's sister. Growing up, my aunt was the mom every child wanted. A stay-at-home mom, room mom, cookie-baking mom, house cleaning mom. Her voice would light up the room, and her laugh was magical. Xavier is also the older brother of my cousin Matt. Matt died when I was eighteen, and I'll never forget seeing my aunt that day in all-black, dark sunglasses. She looked like a scene from a sad movie.

A part of her died that day with my cousin. I think a part of me died that day as well. I didn't have friends growing up. It was complicated with my family, but cousins don't have a choice not to love you, and they're not allowed to judge you. So, Matt was pretty much my best friend. And, if I'm being honest, he and Julie were my only consistent friends.

"I've been by a few times to check on you, but you're never home," Xavier said with a curious half-smile or maybe a judgmental smile. I'm not sure.

"Why didn't you just call? You know I would've made time for you?" I asked.

"What's the fun in that?" he says

"I'm fine," I lie.

"You're a liar."

"Maybe." I shrug.

"So, spill, little cousin."

I roll my eyes. "Where do I start? I just left my husband less than a month or so ago, and I'm in the middle of a divorce. I got a new job that is far more boring than I expected. So much so, I'm considering self-mutilation for enjoyment, and there's a guy."

"*Stop* right there, say no more," he interrupts me. "You already have a crush on a guy at work. It's been a day. Seriously, Harper!" he shouts at me with his hand over his chest and his mouth agape.

"No, I don't have a crush on a guy at work." I give up, throw myself onto my couch, and yell, voice muffled, "Besides, saying it's a crush sounds like we're in middle school. He's a guy at work, and he's infuriating me."

"Why? Because you just left your husband five minutes ago, and you're crushing on him, or because you don't date guys you work or because he's a better salesperson than you?"

"Har, har," I say, very annoyed. I reflect on what I spewed on Xavier, and now I am more confused than ever. Why is he infuriating? Because I can't stop thinking about him? Because everyone likes him, and maybe I'm a little jealous? Am I mad at him, or am I mad at myself for wanting to know this guy? "Why are you here again?"

"To make my favorite cousin call her dad."

I grab my phone and text my dad.

Me —I 'm alive, and I'm not avoiding you. I just started my new job, been busy. I'll call you when I can.

Three bubbles appear and disappear, then reappear.

Xavier and I make ourselves comfortable on my couch, eating all my string cheese and chips and waiting for my dad to reply.

Dad — just wanted to make sure you're good.

My relationship with my dad is complicated. We're not close like I am with my mom. Women loved my dad, or so it seemed, because no one ever said no to him. My dad worked in the fashion industry. He used his looks and charm to get whomever he wanted. And he would cheat on my mom often. His cheating drove a mile-wide divide in our house growing up. I always told myself it was between him and my mom, and it was never any of my business. Sharing a wall with your parents growing up gives a kid more information than they ever need to experience.

There are things parents are supposed to protect their kids from, but I don't feel like I ever got that protection. Walls don't suppress screaming. Vents are gateways for venomous insults and hateful words. I grew numb to it in my teenage years and became interested in the *why* of everything. Why did she stay? Why didn't he leave? Why did she still love him? Why didn't he love her? So, I asked, and my mom told me everything—at least her side of the story.

I've never asked my dad his side, probably because deep down, I know he'd never be honest with me. Or, maybe I don't want to know his truth.

I am still thinking about my dad, but looking at Xavier, I say to Xavier, "You know you look more like my dad than my brother does?"

Dad and Xavier are tall, six foot five inches, and both have olive skin. My dad is very handsome for an older man. And Julie has always told me Xavier is a panty dropper, which makes me want to vomit every time she says it. Both my dad and Xavier have ocean-blue eyes, bordering on clear. That is my favorite feature they share. Their eyes are beautiful.

Xavier puffs up. "Well, that's a compliment because your dad gets all the hot chicks."

I want to be mad at his jab, but it's true.

"Well played," I congratulate him. My dad's infidelity wasn't a secret. Everyone in our extended family knew.

Chapter 7

GABE

Walking into work now, I make it a point to say good morning to Harper first to make up for her first day here when she said I ignored her. I'm sure this makes me look like a love-sick puppy to all the guys because to say hello to her, I have to walk past people's desks and then check back in to say hello to them.

Half the time, she is distracted and doesn't give me the time of day, and the other half, she gives me a courtesy "Morning" without looking up from her computer.

Walking up to her this morning, I see her head is down, and she's frantically banging on her keyboard.

"Good morning," I say, then jokingly add, "Isn't it too early for your keyboard to have pissed you off?"

I chuckle to myself. I always laugh at my jokes. Joy says it's endearing. Landon and Jeff say it's obnoxious. Harper doesn't even respond to me.

I wave my hand in front of her face. "Hey, Earth to Harper."

"What the fuck, Gabe!" she snaps.

"Who pissed in your coffee this morning?" I ask, which, in

hindsight, didn't help her mood in the slightest.

"Fuck off, Gabe!" she seethes.

"Seriously, Harper, it's eight a.m., and you've dropped the F-bomb on me twice in five minutes. What the hell did I do to you now?"

I walked in this morning in a great mood, excited to see Harper. Excited that I get to say good morning to her and watch the different expressions it brings to her face, but today, she's taken all the air from my sails, and I just feel beat down.

She looks up from her computer very slowly, almost as if she's a tiger tracking her next kill, and it's at that moment I know I pissed her off. "Gabe, you are twenty minutes late to work, which means you're twenty minutes behind on emails, which also means you have no idea what is happening. I'm new here, and I have to prove myself. On the other hand, you have five other managers who do the same thing as you do, available to pick up your slack at any given time, so if you'll excuse me, I have a department to run *alone*."

Car dealerships are cutthroat, but Harper takes everything up a level. She's always first to work and the last to leave. The last quarter of the year is when all current-year models must sell. That means there are deals to be made, money to be made, and contests to be won. I like to win. I always win. And I will continue to win at any cost.

When I started as a manager, I was only eighteen years old, straight out of high school. If I wanted anyone to take me seriously, I had to be the best, so I was, and I have no intention of slowing down. Harper can work twenty hours a day and do the work of seven salespeople. She'll still never out-sale me or my sales guys.

Even with all that, though, I'm not a jerk to her. I go out of my way to say good morning; I try to sit by her in meetings and offer her coffee when I go out. I'm trying to be friends with her, but Harper and her blatant disregard for my existence is weighing on me. It's distracting me and making it hard to focus on work. Everyone likes me, and it's killing me that she doesn't. Her icy bullshit attitude is rubbing me the wrong way.

• • •

One day turned into a few days, and a few days turned into a few weeks. She avoids me in the halls, the boardroom, and the breakroom. It's the same thing day after day. When we have our Friday managers' meetings, she makes sure to come in a little later than me so she doesn't have to sit near me. I'm not stupid. I know that she's avoiding me. She's exhausting.

Is it something I said or didn't say? Is she embarrassed about the night I got her out of her car? I need to talk to her, but she walks into the manager's office, greets the others with a cheerful hello, and gives me something closer to a forced half-smile. This situation is getting to the point where we are creating noticeable tension.

Another sales manager, Jeff, must have noticed me watching her walk through the dealership lobby.

"Having a tough time connecting with her?" he asks.

"What?" I ask as he pulls my attention from her.

"You and Harper. You guys avoid each other like the plague. Are you sure you two weren't married in a past life?"

"I just don't get her," I answer honestly.

"Have you thought that maybe you're overthinking everything? Maybe she's exactly what you see. I told you before she's quiet unless it's work-related. She's all work all the time. Ask her for lunch and try to talk to her outside of work," Jeff adds.

"I don't know, she's different with me than you guys," I add. "She's more open with you. She laughs at your jokes. She won't even look me in the eye when she's forced to interact with me, and I don't know why."

Even though deep down inside, I know it must have something to do with that night in her apartment. She has to be hiding something from me. She refuses to let me see her.

"You both bring out the competitive side of each other, so none of us are mad about the tension, but maybe consider what you see is what you get with her and leave it at that," Jeff says as he's walking away.

Chapter 8

Gabe's sulky face when I go into the manager's office and pay him little attention is starting to baffle me. Why is he being so nice to me? He started saying "good morning" to me before anyone else in the office, which is cute but totally unnecessary. He offers to buy me coffee or lunch on any given day. I could ask him for the most random, off-the-wall favor, and he'd do it. Why is he trying so hard to befriend me? I can't let him in, nor do I want to let him in. I don't want to deal with another person in my life.

His constant badgering is driving me crazy. If I befriend him, it won't be as fun when I beat him at every contest. Watching him blow a gasket when I win will be worth every passed-up vanilla latte. Gabe wins every contest, and he has for years. I've been told he's one of the best sales managers they've ever had. But I have to be better.

If I had to guess, he doesn't win for the money or even to gloat about winning. He wins to earn everyone's approval. I win to prove I can win. I win to ensure my department is considered an asset that can't be replaced. I win to make sure when layoffs happen (and they are inevitable), that I'm not on the chopping block. I know I'm not warm and fuzzy. I'm genuine and truthful. I'm honest and I care.

Gabe's advantage over me is everyone falls at his feet. Gabe innocently flirts with the young receptionists so they'll feed his team walk-ins, and they play right into him. Watching this infuriates me, but I pretend I'm none the wiser. The older ladies in the business office give him googly eyes and always say, "Whatever you need, Gabe, anything for you, Gabe."

When other managers ask for something, all we get is a dismissive response like, "That will take a few days, or look it up yourself." To get their dirty work done, certain managers began offering Gabe a free lunch as a bribe to handle tasks in the business office for them. Despite this, I refuse to ask him for help.

Watching him charm the older ladies and flirt with the younger girls to get what he wants makes his early morning hellos and lunch offers disingenuous, and I do not trust anything he does. Gabe thinks he deserves my attention. Gabe is happy and friendly, but I am not those things. I am cordial and reserved. Gabe has fun at work. I work at work. Gabe sees the best in everyone, but I am skeptical. He was an only child, or maybe the baby with older siblings. Whichever one, he and I have nothing in common.

A few hours into my day, I see the reflection of someone standing behind me. I immediately know it's him. I can smell his cologne as it invades my cubical. It's the same scent from the first morning: tobacco and citrus. When I sit in the chair he spent the night in, I can still faintly smell it. Unknowingly, I take a deep breath, and you can see my chest rise.

"Do you like it?" he asks, full of arrogance.

With furrowed brows, I turn around and say, "Excuse me?"

"My cologne he says, I saw you inhale when I came up behind you."

"I didn't notice your cologne," I lie. "What do you need, Gabe?"

I'm assuming the frustration that's coursing through my veins is evident when I talk because he quickly retorts,

"I'm kidding, I come in peace." He takes my chair and spins me around to look at him, but that spin lands me perfectly at eye level with his crotch. I can't help but look. Noticing his mishap, he turns and sits next to me on my desk with his legs stretched out in front of him. He's still a bit higher than me, forcing me to look up at him. His eyes are dark brown, so dark they're bottomless. They refuse to let anyone in. It's almost like looking into a well.

"I wanted to invite you to lunch. I see you eat here every day, and I thought I'd treat you to something other than a salad," he says.

"Thanks, but I have work to do," I reply too quickly, and my suspicious tone makes him ask me again.

"Harper, you can tell me no a thousand times, and I'll continue to ask until you say yes. I'm not the number one sales manager because I give up. I will wear you down sooner than later."

"Good to know," I say, crossing my arms over my chest.

"Listen, it's just lunch. You've been here for a few months, and we haven't spoken more than ten words to each other," he says, and I wonder what happened to the confident, "I'm the number one sales manager, and I get what I want," guy? He continues, almost begging, "You're a very hard person to read, Harper. I'm genuinely just trying to get to know you."

His words make my chest tighten, and I hate myself for feeling like this when he's near me.

As he leans against my desk, legs close enough that if I swayed one way too far, we'd touch, I can't help but feel warmer inside rather than the coldness I'm accustomed to.

Why is he being so nice to me right now?

"I'm swamped today, Gabe. Today just isn't a good day."

He throws his arms up, and it's hard not to laugh. "Please,"

Before I can answer, he says in a low, pleading voice, "Harper, come on." And I think I'm melting inside.

My stomach starts to negotiate with my brain. It's just lunch. I'm not overly hungry, but I forgot my salad, so today is as good a day as any to have lunch with him.

Before my mind can say no, my mouth says, "Fine."

Dammit, my brain never wins, and we all know my mouth never listens to my brain and says whatever the hell it wants to anyway.

That's all it took for him to grab me by the wrist and drag me to his car.

"Umm...You know it's eleven, right?" I question.

"I skipped breakfast," he says, and I know he's lying.

"Seriously, Gabe, why are we rushing to your car?"

He stops and looks at me, almost admitting defeat, "Harper, you won't look me in the eye for more than three seconds; you haven't spoken more than twenty words since we've met. You've agreed to go to lunch with me, and I'm not allowing a second to pass for you to change your mind. So, we're going to lunch early. We'll have more time to get to know each other."

I think that last part was intended to be a joke, but I know he's dead serious.

"Okay, get to know each other during lunch hour. This should be interesting," I say as I roll my eyes and allow him to pull me behind him.

Chapter 9

We pull into a parking space in front of a restaurant I have never heard of in a part of town I have never been to. It is a prominent Mexican restaurant with an orange and white exterior and insufficient windows for natural light.

Walking in, I am overwhelmed by the smell of fajitas, and, as I guessed from the exterior, it is dark. We sit in a small booth across from each other. Gabe orders water, taquitos, and an enchilada. Despite my lack of appetite, I decide to order the tortilla soup. Sitting across from him makes any previous hunger turn to nerves.

I need clarification about why we were here, and my guard is higher than usual. Growing up, I didn't have more than a friend or two at a time. I refused to open up and let people in. I never felt good enough for the kids I wanted to be friends with. I was embarrassed by my parents and our home. I was too average, which is what I told myself, but I think that was more to keep myself safe from judgment or rejection than true.

"Tell me about yourself," Gabe says.

"Seriously," I say. "We're doing this?"

"Doing what?" he questions.

"Small talk."

"Well, isn't that why we're here?" he asks, so fun-loving that I don't know if this is genuine Gabe or showy-work Gabe.

"I don't know why you're here, but I'm here to eat something other than a salad," I say jokingly. Then I add, "I'm twenty-four years old, I was born and raised in Southern California, I have one older brother, and I've been working since I was sixteen years old."

"Hmmmmm. That was deep stuff, Harper," he says, looking up from his food but not lifting his head to make eye contact.

"Well, what are you asking me? What exactly are you fishing for?" I know my tone is a little too harsh for what he's asking, so I take a deep breath and try not to be so defensive.

"Nothing specific. I just wanted to learn a little about you."

"Do you take all new hires out to lunch?" I question.

"Only if they're as pretty as you are," he says matter-of-factly, and I can feel my cheeks turn scarlet. Why is he being so nice right now?

"Seriously, Gabe, that was unprofessional," I joke.

"We're not at work," he retorts.

I feel him trying to peek over my walls, and I cannot let that happen. We work together. This needs to stay professional. I have too much to prove. I can't get mixed up in office drama, and let's not forget I literally just left my husband.

"Tell me about you," I say, trying to take the attention off me.

"I'm twenty-nine years old, I was born and raised in West Covina, I don't have any siblings, and I've been working since I was fifteen."

"Ha, I knew it," I say, way too excited.

"You knew what?" His brows are furrowed, and he has a half smile. He knows there's more to my statement.

"I knew you were the only child." He gives me a questioning

look. "I meant to say I assumed you were an only child." He nods his head, telling me he doesn't appreciate my opinion. So, I'm honest with him. "Gabe, only children are spoiled. They crave attention. That's my perception of you. I'm not saying it's bad. It's just my experience."

"You have no idea who I am, Harper. And your flawed view of only children is bullshit."

He's defensive, maybe even annoyed with me, but dammit, when he says my name, I forget everything around me.

"Can we talk about the elephant in the room?" he asks as he changes the subject, clearly not wanting to engage with me about his childhood.

"About how I'm going to beat you at every sales contest at work?"

"Nope, not that elephant," he says seriously. "The other elephant."

"About how I'm a better manager than you?"

He visibly stifles a grin. "Nope, not that one either."

"I'm all out of elephants," I say with a smile and a shrug. If he thinks I'm volunteering any information about that night, he's crazy.

His stare is serious now. "Can I ask why I found you passed out in your car that day?"

I squirm a little in my seat. I take a deep breath and let it out.

"I was just exhausted," I lie.

His drawn-in brows don't hide the fact that there is no way he believes me.

"That's God's truth," I lie again.

He doesn't stop glaring at me with discernment in his eyes, and I know he is not letting me off the hook without the full truth. He's been waiting too long for my clipped half-truth.

Begrudgingly, I admit, "I left my husband a week or so earlier and had to move my things from there to my new apartment. It was a lot physically and emotionally."

Saying this aloud makes me feel less sad than I imagined it would. I never really loved Liam. It was a marriage of convenience. He was my ticket out of my parents' house at eighteen. I never thought we'd get married, but he asked, and I felt obligated to say yes. It's the natural progression. It's what everyone expected. The reality of leaving him wasn't my issue. The failed marriage is what stings the most.

He looks at me with wide eyes, clearly shocked. "Shit, Harper, I'm so sorry."

"Don't pity me, Gabe. I decided to leave. There's no climactic backstory. Just two people who should've never been married," I say, trying to control my emotions that, at this point, are all over the place.

"I don't pity you, Harper. I actually respect you for not being afraid to do what is right for you. I pity the sorry guy who fell in love with you and got his heart broken. A girl like you only comes around once in a lifetime."

I blush for the second time this lunch. *He is not shy about saying what is on his mind, is he?* I smile at him because what else do I say? Thank you? No, that's weird. Why would he say something so vulnerable? Where is the happy-go-lucky business office charmer? The life-of-the-party guy?

Trying to lighten the mood and change the subject from my failed marriage and his once-in-a-lifetime girl comment, I spew out like a child, "Oh, and I thought I was taking an ibuprofen, but I took a sleeping pill instead." Then, quickly add, "I was listening to the radio, lost in thought, and fell asleep." I break our eye contact and stir my now lukewarm soup as I bite the inside of my cheek. "I know, pretty stupid," I add. Why am I sharing all this with him?

"Not stupid. But the next time you decide to take a sleeping pill, can you wait until you're in your apartment," he says with a laugh.

I give him a salute and say, "Yes, sir!"

After that, we fall into normal light conversation. I take a deep breath and try to take in the moment. Gabe is not at my apartment watching me sleep, nor are we harboring that secret anymore. We've talked about it, and there's no more fear of judgment. It is what it is now. He knows my truth and seems okay with it. That's a huge weight off my shoulders.

Pulling back into our work parking lot, I look at my watch.

"Shit, Gabe, we've been gone for a while!" I cry.

"So?" he says in a huff. "According to office gossip, you call all the shots."

"I'm not worried about getting in trouble for being gone too long. I'm worried about what everyone will say when they figure out who I've been gone with for so long," I say with a grin.

"Managers go to lunch all the time, Harper," he retorts.

"Not you and me, Gabe," I argue. "You and I have everyone watching our tension-filled interactions every time we pass in the hall. There will be plenty of questions. You know that as well as I do."

He pulls in his cheek and smirks, highlighting his dimple. He doesn't smile but smirks, and I can read every thought behind it. I get out of the car and hurry back into the dealership.

I look over my shoulder, wink and say, "Hey Gabe, thanks for lunch. It was good getting out, even if it was with you."

While I try to sound sarcastic, unfortunately, it was genuinely great getting to know him, and that scares the hell out of me.

He laughs and flashes me his panty-dropping dimple smile.

Chapter 10

When I get home, Xavier is cooking in my apartment. I inhale deeply and sigh as I take in the smell of bread. I love bread. If I could live on carbs and not gain weight, my entire diet would consist of some version of bread. Xavier knows about my love for carbs and doesn't care how it affects my waistline.

I've always had body dysmorphia. My brother used to say I was overweight, and I believed him. My modeling agency told me I was too big. Once they stopped telling me I was overweight, I started telling myself. I'm not fat. My better judgment tries to talk sense into me daily. I'm not a size zero. I'll never be a size zero, and even if I were a zero, there would be something else.

"How did you get into my apartment?" I ask.

"Hello, my favorite cousin; dinner smells amazing!" he says sarcastically, mimicking my voice and doing a terrible job.

"Honey, I'm home. By the aroma encompassing my apartment, you're making carbs for dinner. Why are you here?" I ask again.

"Ha ha ha. Sit down," he says, pulling out my chair. "Dinner is done, and I'm starving."

"Okay, but seriously, how did you get in, and why are you here?"

"I'm here because I was bored, and I made a copy of your key a few days ago and needed to test it to make sure it worked in case there's an emergency," he says as if the fact he stole my spare to make himself one is just okay.

"You're bored, that's it? Why didn't you call? What if I had plans, Xavier?"

He spits out his whisky and starts choking uncontrollably. If he weren't such an ass, I would've been worried, but if he died right now, I'm not sure I'd cry.

"Let me know when you're finished," I say dryly.

Still choking in between words, he manages to get out. "You and plans is an oxymoron; you know that, right, Harper? You have no friends besides me, and if we're being honest, we were forced to like each other."

"I have Julie, too," I say as I puff out my chest.

He pats my hand, mocking me. "You have Julie, too."

He's not wrong, but it still stings to hear. I have two people in this world I can depend on. I couldn't even depend on Liam when I had him. I'm unsure if anyone else would be as honest with me as Xavier and Julie.

Sitting at dinner, drinking our favorite alcohol, and eating our weight in pasta, we're just real with each other. "Do you think all cousins are like us?" I ask, twirling another bite of pasta around my fork.

"No," he answers without explanation.

I raise my eyebrows, surprised by his clipped answer.

Unphased by my reaction, he continues, "You just left your husband, and hot work guy is off limits. We all know you don't break the rules, so what plans could you have?"

I sit briefly and formulate a snarky reply, but he's right. I'm not a rule-breaker by nature. Growing up, I didn't have many rules because my parents were terrible at keeping track of my brother and me.

Changing the subject from my sorry love life, I ask Xavier, "Remember that day when I was in fifth grade, and I took the long way home from school?"

He answers, "How can I forget your mom standing in the middle of the street, screaming and then falling to her knees crying? That is a visual that will be burned in my head forever."

That day, I took the long way home from school, and my mom thought I had gotten kidnapped. She made a scene that none of our neighbors will ever forget.

"Why were you even there?" I ask.

"The middle school was off that day, so I was hanging out with your brother. My parents knew your mom was teetering on the edge of a nervous breakdown for a while. Your dad wasn't shy about sharing. They wanted me there to help with you, I guess." He shrugs at me because neither of us really knows why he was there.

I continue my story, "All it took was a longer-than-usual walk home, and there she was, having a complete mental breakdown in the middle of our street for the entire neighborhood to witness. That is just one of a hundred reasons I didn't have friends. Could you imagine walking home with a friend to that scene? No, thank you."

Xavier says, "Your brother was so embarrassed. He stayed with us for a week after that day. I don't think he ever wanted to come home."

I lean forward over the table and ask, "Do you blame him?"

"No, but you never left. You stayed there to make sure your mom would be okay." He gives me a pitying smile.

"Mom was placed on administrative leave, which made her more depressed. She spent weeks in bed. I'd clean while she spent days hiding in her bedroom. I hated that house. It was always dark, but those weeks exaggerated the dungeon feel we were all forced to live in. There was little natural light." I say, looking to the ceiling, remembering the feeling of coming home to that house.

"Dark wood cabinets lined our windowless kitchen, dark carpet covered our floors, and dark drapes covered our few windows. It was cold in the summer and freezing in the winter. The house was quiet. Everyone did their part to avoid each other. At that point, it was the easiest way. The less my brother and I interacted, the less we fought, and the less stress we caused our mom."

"You're killing my buzz with your pity party, Harper," Xavier huffs, which quickly snaps me out of my terrible trip down dysfunction lane.

"Sorry," I regrettably admit. "Somedays, I can't help it."

Rubbing his belly, Xavier says, "Dinner was amazing if I don't say so myself. The conversation was a five out of ten, but only because you stopped telling me about hot work guy."

I try to pour more wine into my glass only to realize we have already drunk it. Panic takes over Xavier as he says, "Tell me you have more wine hidden somewhere. This was the only bottle I could find."

I throw my head back and laugh. "It's really sad I have to hide wine from my cousin, who isn't supposed to have a key to my apartment. Of course, I have more wine. But you need to close your eyes while I get it."

"Harper, this apartment is the size of a shoebox. You can't pee without your neighbors hearing."

I wince at his visual. "Ew, that's terrible. It's in the coat closet in the bin on the left side."

"You need to learn to share, Harper," he teases as he makes

his way over to the closet and grabs not one but two bottles of wine. It's going to be a rough morning.

A few hours and a lot of wine later, I slur, "Xavier, you're going to make one lucky girl happy one day."

"Hopefully, it's one of the hot girls in your apartment building," he jokes.

"And now I have the truth!" I exclaim. "Xavier Parson, you are at my apartment more than your own because of all the hot girls."

He tries to shove me, but the wine has clouded his ability to measure our distance. He falls over, hanging off my dining chair with his head resting on my floor. "You seriously didn't think it was to hang out with my grouchy cousin, did you? It's for the view from the balcony."

He's laughing, and I know he's not lying.

"You're a creeper," I mock him.

"No, Harper, I'm a single guy who isn't allowed to date their cousin's best friend, so I'm forced to people-watch from her apartment."

"Yuck, Xavier. I'm going to bed. I can't engage in a conversation about you and Julie. I'm too drunk, and I may say things I'll regret tomorrow. Goodnight." I huff as I turn to leave him with three empty bottles of wine and unwashed dishes everywhere.

"Hey!" he yells at me as I'm walking away. "You need to clean up dinner. I cooked it, you clean it. That's our deal!"

"Goodnight, Xavier." I groan from down my hall.

Chapter 11

I wake up too early for a Saturday morning with a throbbing headache.

"*Xavier, are you still here?*" I yell from my bedroom to the living room, where I left a very wine-drunk Xavier last night at some ungodly hour.

"Stop yelling," I hear his stifled groan. His face must be buried in a pillow.

"I'm hungry," I yell.

"I'm hungover," he yells back.

I drag myself out of bed and zombie walk to the living room, where Xavier is half on and half off my couch. "You look terribly uncomfortable."

"Don't judge me," he begs. "Half the night, I was too drunk to care, and the other half, I was too hungover to do anything about it.

"Get up, brush your teeth, let's go to breakfast," I order.

"You're a bad influence," he complains.

"You're a featherweight when it comes to drinking, and you always have been." I poke at him. "There's only one way to cure a hangover. Greasy food."

"Well, some of us didn't start drinking in the womb, Harper."

We both laugh.

I started drinking during my first year of high school. When I say drinking, I mean falling drunk every weekend. I did it to quiet the voice in my head. At parties, the fear of being judged didn't stop at my appearance. It festered and grew into every part of my life. What if I said something stupid at a party? What if someone didn't think I belonged there? Every week, there was a new excuse to drink.

I eventually stopped looking for excuses and embraced being drunk as my default setting. This drunken state of mind lasted almost six years, including the entire year of my marriage. Once I saw myself turning into my parents by hiding from reality through alcohol or substance abuse, I stopped. Once I stopped, I realized how toxic my marriage was and left.

Teeth brushed, hair brushed, I grabbed Xavier, who had found his way back to my couch, yanked him up by the wrist, and headed out for our greasy breakfast.

The elevator dings, doors open, and when I look up to step in, I see him...

"Gabe," I say, way too surprised, or did I sound excited?

Shit, I hope I don't sound excited. I feel a bit of embarrassment rush over my cheeks. I look hungover, and he looks like he just walked out of Hot Neighbor Magazine. Seriously, it's just my luck.

"Harper," he stammers for a second. He knows I live here, so why is he surprised to see me?

"Hi, I'm Joy," comes the sweetest little voice beside him. "Do you know each other?"

Gabe stammers for a second time and answers, "Yes, we work together. Harper just started a few months ago."

My mind goes wild seeing the two of them together. Gabe didn't tell me he had a girlfriend when we were at lunch less than forty-eight hours ago. What an asshole. I knew I couldn't trust him. Any guy who asks a co-worker to lunch and doesn't mention his girlfriend is trouble.

"Oh, how great! A friend from work in my building, maybe we can..." She looks between Xavier and myself. "...have dinner sometime."

I look up at Xavier and roll my eyes. He, in turn, gives me a big smile, letting me know he can read how uncomfortable (and hungry) I am. He is clearly enjoying every second of this awkward interaction.

"Yeah, that would be great," Xavier answers politely. "Dinner," he parrots what she said, laughs, and puts his arm around my neck.

Irritated, I rush into the elevator so the doors don't close, leaving us stranded there with Gabe and his perky sidekick.

Gabe gives Xavier the once over and says, "I didn't catch your name."

Xavier lets the doors close without answering.

Walking to breakfast, I feel the weight of Xavier's stare on my head.

"We work together, Xavier. It's the guy I was telling you about. The one that infuriates me. The one from work." I huff and throw up my arms. "Were you not listening to anything I said last night?"

"Oh yes, I was listening, but watching you meltdown about hot work boyfriend is just too good." He laughs and grabs my arm. "He likes you, and you like him," Xavier says in his best fifteen-year-old girl voice.

"Stop it. I don't have a crush on him. We don't get along, and it appears he has a girlfriend he failed to mention on multiple occasions."

"Well, to him and his very pretty little sidekick, it looks like you have a boyfriend, and the last time I checked, marrying your first cousin isn't legal in the great state of California."

I punch him in the kidney.

"Seriously." He moans, hunched over, grabbing his left side. "Why don't you like him?" He manages under his escaping breath.

"He's a pick-me guy. He has to win every contest and tries to charm all the women at work to do whatever he asks. And it works. Everyone falls to their feet. I take pride in being the only one that doesn't ogle over him."

"Ohhhhh, so he's the male version of you. And since you've never really liked who you are, you hate the male version of you just as bad, if not worse."

"You have a lot to say, Xavier, for a man I had to drag off my couch not one minute ago. Don't make me call your mom."

Chapter 12

Monday morning comes too soon, and I want to be anywhere but here at work. I play the weekend over and over in my head. I drank way too much with Xavier on Friday. Running into Gabe outside the elevator on Saturday morning didn't help things. I figured running into him was inevitable since he said he was my neighbor, sort of. Isn't it enough I have to see him at work, why at home too?

Unable to concentrate on work, I shoot a text to Xavier.

Me – Had fun this weekend; you still didn't tell me how you got into my apartment, though.

Xavier – I told you already; you must've been drunk. I had a key made. I had fun, too. I'm telling my mom you made me drink too much, and you're corrupting me.

Me – She'll believe you if you do, and you won't be able to hang out with me anymore.

Xavier – I know that's the point. Tell boy crush I said hi, and I can't wait for our double dinner date.

Me – You're an ass!

I hear yelling from across the dealership, so I put my phone away and look up to see what is happening. Of course, it's Gabe. No one else yells across the entire dealership like they're on a playground.

"We're going for drinks tonight after work," I hear him shouting from across the room. I ignore him, assuming he's not talking to me.

"Harper!" he exclaims.

I look down at my computer now, trying to avoid eye contact.

"What?" I ask, annoyed.

"Did you hear me?"

"Uh yeah, sorry, I thought you were talking to someone else." I start to type aimlessly on my computer, trying to look busy.

"Well…"

"Well, what?"

"Drinks tonight. Are you even listening?"

No, I tell myself I'm not listening to him. Every time this man talks to me, it does something inside me. I'm trying my hardest to keep him at arm's length, but he makes it nearly impossible when he talks to me. I just got out of a relationship that lasted almost my entire adult life thus far. We met when I was eighteen and moved in together almost immediately. I stayed with him because I knew that's what was expected of me. Then, just months ago, I left him.

It's too early to start a relationship with someone new, and the last person I'm getting involved with is Gabe from work. I run away from every friendship opportunity as well as relationship opportunity. I've kept one person in my life who's not family, and that's Julie. My failure rate with relationships is 99%. I'm not about to test my odds with someone from work.

Pulling myself out of my thoughts, I finally answer, "Sorry, I can't make it. Maybe next time?"

"Why not, hot date?" he asks. I'm assuming he's fishing for information on Xavier, who is not a date or boyfriend but a very annoying cousin.

Looking up from my desk, I scrunch my nose and say, "You know it's Monday, right? And why the hell are we yelling at each other across the office? You know you can come to my desk and talk to me," I continue to yell across the office.

We are so unprofessional.

Before those words leave my mouth, I already regret saying them. He turns in my direction and starts to walk over.

"Fuck," I mutter under my breath. *Why, Harper, why do you even open your mouth?*

He smells expensive. All the guys at work smell great, but Gabe smells expensive. He exudes confidence, and it drives me crazy. He's dangerous. This whole thing could get messy if I don't keep my guard up. Sitting with one leg on my desk and one leg on the floor, he looks me over.

"Can I help you?" I ask.

"Who's your boyfriend? You didn't mention him at lunch."

"Ummm, not my boyfriend," I say, trying not to laugh. "And, back at you, who's your little bundle of sunshine?"

A glimmer of something shows in his dark brown eyes. I can't distinguish if it's guilt or arrogance. Is it guilt because I caught him in a lie or arrogance because he caught me jealous of his girlfriend? Frustration stirs in my belly, but I don't break eye contact with him. I'm not sure I've ever seen more dark and captivating eyes than his.

"It never came up," he snaps.

"What never came up?" I ask, shaking my head, confused because I've apparently lost my ability to focus when he looks at me.

"My *not* girlfriend. Good God, girl, do you pay attention to anything?"

Not when I look into your eyes, I say in the privacy of my mind, but then quickly retort out loud, "I only pay attention to things worth paying attention to." With that insult, I look back at my computer and start to type.

"Ok, you win," he says, holding his hands up in surrender. "I'm sorry."

"I always win, Gabe. What game we play determines how hard I'll try."

I look at him, and he's staring at me, like staring into my soul. As much as I'm trying to shut him out, I can't. I feel like all my feelings are on display.

"Drinks, Harper. How do I get you to join us for drinks?" he says, putting his hands together at his chest, begging me for the answer he wants.

"I'm busy."

"All the time?"

"Pretty much."

"You're impossible."

"You're a quick study."

When he finally accepts defeat and stands to leave, I shoot him a quick wink and say, "Oh, and my boyfriend isn't my boyfriend. He's my cousin, and his name is Xavier. So, you can tell your perky little *not* girlfriend not to plan any double dinner dates."

"Wait, what?" he says. His tone indicates confusion.

It probably wasn't the best time to tell him about Xavier, but this is what Gabe does to me. He makes me mad, jealous, and insane at the same time, and it's so different from anything I've ever experienced. I look down at my computer, trying to convey to him I no longer want to have this very public conversation with him at the dealership. Apparently, getting the hint, he lowers his head and walks away. And I don't miss any of his frustration.

Me – Hey, do you want to meet me for drinks tonight? I got invited and need a buffer or a wingman.

Xavier – Who invited you? I have to work late. :|

Me – NOOOO!!! I need you. Gabe asked if I wanted to go.

Xavier – Don't yell at me. It's not my fault I have to work, and your work boyfriend is pocking holes in your armor.

Me – UGHHHHH! I feel like a jerk continuing to turn down everyone's invites.

Xavier – Everyone's invites or Gabe's invites.

Before I can answer, there's another text from Xavier

Xavier – You could go home. But we all know boy crush will be at the bar, and there's no way you'll allow yourself to be left out without a reason. Have fun. Make friends! :D

Me – I can't go, I don't want to go.

Xavier – You don't want to go alone. You're torn between no one is allowed close to me, and I don't want to be left out of everything and die alone. You need a buffer. Use Boy Crush as a buffer. I'm sure he won't mind.

Me – Bye.

I can't say his last text isn't spot-on. I've been battling with not wanting friends and not wanting to be left out my entire life. Even worse, I don't know how to change it.

Chapter 13

I pace outside the bar for five minutes, trying to talk myself out of going inside, and then another five minutes to talk myself into going inside. The overwhelming feeling of doom deep in my stomach is messing with my head. If I go in, it'll be the start of something I don't want to be part of. Drinks with co-workers are never just drinks. It's friendships and questions. That's something I want no part of.

Growing up, it was Julie and me against the world. That idealism has served me well. She protected me from the judgment of other kids in school. I don't enjoy answering questions about my personal life, no matter how surface-level they may be. The longer I stand out here, the longer I'm here. Wiping my sweating palms down my jeans, I turn and walk in.

"Vodka cranberry!" I yell across the bar at the very handsome, fit, tall, dark-haired, blue-eyed bartender who also seemed to notice me.

I tried to start a tab, but he said, "It's on me," and my suspicions were confirmed. I have a bar-boyfriend, and I may let him take me home tonight.

I cross to the table where a few co-workers are chatting about life outside of work, and I can't help but try to fade into the corner. I'm awkward in social settings, but as a manager, making an appearance to drink is important, not only to me but to all of them. It's their way of finding common ground.

Some people are natural at making small talk. I am a natural salesperson. There is a difference. I can talk about sales strategies, cars, and E-commerce all day long, but I was not blessed with the gift of small talk, and we all know none of these people are here to talk about sales strategies. Gabe, on the other hand, has the gift of gab. He's so good at just talking to people about random things.

Gabe touches my arm as he appears behind me. "Hey, want to grab a table outside?" My body heats at his touch.

His chest is pressed against my back as he loudly whispers in my ear so I can hear him above all the bar noise. As he holds me there, waiting for my answer, I swear time stands still. Gabe comes around to look at me, a wave of relief rushes over me. Tonight, he can be my escape from my social insecurities.

I wave my arm toward the bar and say. "I can't. My bartender boyfriend will get jealous."

Gabe looks at me and then quickly to the hot bartender, shakes his head, and says, "Seriously?"

I laugh, grab his arm, and lead him outside. Once we're free of all the noise, I say, "You're way too easy to play. For a top sales manager, your poker face sucks."

There's a minute of uncomfortable silence, and I realize I don't do well in silence when Gabe is around. If I'm being honest with myself, I don't do well in silence when he isn't around either.

"So, your *not* girlfriend is pretty," I declare, not knowing what else to say.

"Harper, I swear Joy and I are just friends. We used to..." He pauses and then thoughtfully proceeds, "We used to date.

We were never exclusive." he looks at me for my reaction.

"What changed?" I ask with one brow raised.

He looks confused at my question. "What do you mean?"

"I'm just wondering what changed between your last non-exclusive hook-up and now. What made you decide to be just friends?"

I hate myself right now for asking him about her. I try to tell myself that I don't care, but I do care. Why do I care? This is none of my business.

"What changed?" he repeats my question aloud to no one. Then he taps his chin as if he's deep in thought for effect and answers, "I guess work had a little to do with our mutual parting."

He looks so smug right now. He thinks I'm jealous. Shit, am I jealous? I can't be jealous. I can't stand this guy.

"So, you were friends with benefits?" I ask. I need to stop talking. Why can't I stop? I shouldn't care who she is.

"We *were* friends with benefits, but *now* we're just friends." He leans back in his chair and crosses his arms. His sleeves come up to his elbows. No man should have forearms like that.

I raise my eyebrows, slightly surprised by his cold answer, and ask, "Just like that?"

"Just like that." Another clipped answer. It's obvious he's done with this line of questioning.

"I'm not judging you, Gabe. I just don't do friendships or relationships. I needed to leave my parent's house right after high school, so I moved in with my now ex-husband because I thought he would take care of me. When I was willing to admit he and I were as dysfunctional as what I was running away from, I left him, and here I am." *Shit*, why did I say all that? See, I'm terrible at this *let's have a drink* thing. Alcohol is a truth serum for me. It always wins! "Ummm, I'm so sorry that I just unloaded all that on you. It was very inappropriate of me to tell you all that. I don't know if it's the alcohol or you. I guess you're just easy to talk to..."

He reaches out his right hand to shake mine, chuckles, and says, "That is the most authentic thing you've said to me since we met. Nice to finally meet you, Harper Atwood."

"Gabe, why are you so nice to me? I have given you zero reasons to continue to try to be friends with me, and you keep coming back for more abuse."

He drinks his beer slowly and then sets it on the table beside him so there's no obstruction between us. He leans forward on his elbows and bites his cheek as he studies me. I can see his dimple, and damn that dimple, the things it makes me want to do.

"Because I like you," he says.

Shaking my head, I ask, "What?"

"Because I like you. You asked why I'm still nice to you even though you're a bitch to me." He smiles.

"Ummm, I don't think I used those words."

"Didn't you?" he questions.

Starting to feel a little uncomfortable with this weird feeling building inside me, I suggest, "Maybe we should go inside and mingle with everyone."

"You're probably right," he reluctantly agrees, and I don't miss the disappointment in his voice.

After a few hours chatting with everyone from work and a few too many drinks later, I'm talking a little louder than I usually do and leaning on the tables more relaxed than I should be.

"Shit, I'm drunk!" I say with a slur to Gabe. "I think I need to go. I'm going to call an Uber."

Heroically, he replies, "I'll take you. It's not like I don't know where you live, and I'm going there anyway." I glare at him. "It's not like that, Harper. We are friends," I continue to glare at him.

"No, it's fine. I'll call an Uber. Or my cousin. You remember my cousin," I say, laughing at my joke way harder than necessary. Yep, I'm drunk.

"Seriously, Harper, stop being such a pain in my ass all the time. I'm offering you a ride." His jaw twitches, and I know he's pissed. "Take it."

"Okay, okay, no need to scold the drunk girl," I slur.

We park in the visitor's area of the parking garage, so I'm a little turned around, but it's not like I can see much anyway. My world is spinning.

"Where are we?" I ask, trying to get my bearings.

"In your parking garage, are you sure you'll be okay? Do you need me to walk you up to your apartment? I know where it is," he jokes.

I look at him, roll my eyes, and say, "Thanks for driving me tonight."

"You're welcome," he says softly.

I open my door, but he grabs my arm and pulls me back into the car. I'm so close to him that I can feel his breath on my face, and my body temperature instantly rises twenty degrees.

"Wait!" I warn him, "You do not want to do this."

"How do you know what I want Harper?"

The rise and fall of my chest is noticeable at this point, and if this continues, I'm going to have to sober up quicker than I wanted to because no one has ever made a good decision after four vodka cranberries.

"I'm a mistake, Gabe, a big mistake. I'm not the girl who stays in someone's life. I come in and then leave, giving myself just enough time to fuck everything up." Then I say in a very unsteady voice, "I'm a shitty friend Gabe and an even worse girlfriend."

"Harper, I didn't ask you to be my girlfriend," he says with zero emotion, and his eyes are no longer brown; they're black and void of emotion.

Why does my name sound so good leaving his mouth? Whenever he says it, I feel my walls crack just a little.

He continues, "Are you trying to ensure I'm not catching feelings for you?"

"Exactly," I say, still looking away.

I feel foolish saying all this now. Of course, he doesn't want anything with me. He was sleeping with a girl that he wasn't committed to. Why would I tell him I'm a shitty girlfriend? My stomach feels like a washing machine, and all that alcohol I drank tonight is threatening to re-appear.

"I have to go, Gabe. I can't do this with you tonight."

"Do What? Harper, you're overreacting," he says.

"Gabe, that's what I do. That's who I am. I overreact, I overthink, I say stupid shit, and I regret it five minutes later. I tried to warn you. Seriously, if I don't get fresh air, I'm going to vomit in your car."

And that's all it took for him to finally free me from a very awkward conversation. Once in my apartment, I turn my shower to the hottest setting I can take and try to wash the last twenty minutes off my body along with the buzz from earlier tonight.

Once dried off and in bed, my phone lights up.

Xavier – you alive?

Me – LOL, I'm alive.

Xavier – did you have fun?

Me – NO!

Me – Why don't you remind me how much I hate social gatherings?

Me – of all nights for you to sleep at home, you had to choose tonight.

Xavier – open your door.

I jump up and run to the door. Slowly cracking it open, I see my cousin. He's wearing black joggers and a bright blue hoodie that brings out his sky-blue eyes.

"You have no idea how happy I am to see you," I say.

As I feel the world around me spin, I realize I'm still buzzed from drinking with Gabe.

"Awhhh, is my ice princess melting in my presence."

"Shut up!" I joke as I slap his chest, trying not to stumble into him.

"Do you think I'd miss out on the aftermath of your first night out with new co-workers' drama?"

"Are you thirsty?" I ask.

"Yeah, just water," he answers, and I use the fridge door to hold me up as I grab two waters.

Handing him his bottle, I say, "I need water too. I had way too much to drink tonight."

"How did you get home?"

"Gabe," I tell him.

"Your boyfriend?" he questions with too much curiosity and a smug smile on his face.

"Not my boyfriend, Xavier, remember? I don't do boyfriends, but there was a hot bartender."

"Stop right there, no bartenders. Ever."

"Okay, okay," I say with my hands up in surrender.

"But seriously, Harper, Gabe already has a girlfriend."

"I know. Technically, they're friends with benefits, and as of recently, just friends and no benefits, but that doesn't matter because, unlike you, I don't care about Gabe or his sidekick."

"Who are you trying to convince me or you?"

"Let's talk on the balcony," I insist. "I need some fresh air."

"I'm not done talking about this, Harper," he says, following on my heels.

I fall onto one of my balcony chairs and prop my feet on the railing. "Xavier, what do you want from me?"

"The truth," he says emphatically.

I put my head between my legs as if I'm preparing myself for a plane crash. The rush of blood to my head magnifies my buzz, and it takes me a minute to gather my thoughts.

With my head still hanging between my legs, I give Xavier my truth. "I can't allow myself to like this guy."

"You've said that a million and one times, Harper. Sit up and tell me why."

"First of all, I just left Liam, and he's got this weird friendship thing going on with that girl."

"What is the acceptable timeframe to move on?" he asks.

"I don't know, Xavier. I'm new at this."

"Exactly, there isn't one. Next excuse," he retorts.

"Second, we work together, and that reason alone is enough not to get involved with Gabe. Workplace romance is not an option for me. You know how important my job is to me. I'm not letting some guy who is, I'll admit, super-hot jeopardize it. Third, we're too different. He's a lover boy. *Everyone needs to love me. Please pick me*, and I'm not. He cares too much about what everyone thinks about him."

"Wait, wait, wait." Xavier interrupts me. "You're telling me you don't like him because he cares about how people perceive him?"

"Yes," I say, insistent.

"Are you kidding me right now? I have never met anyone more afraid of others' judgment than you, and now you're calling out someone for sharing your insecurities. Harper, you have one friend because you're afraid to put yourself out there. You have always told yourself you're not worthy of friendship. You are afraid of rejection, so you settled for Liam straight out of high school, and you, till this day, make zero effort in social settings." Xavier is jumping up and down to point out how crazy he thinks I am. I glare at him. "Tell me I'm wrong, Harper. Tell me being judged by others isn't your biggest insecurity!" he insists.

"You're not wrong," I whisper-shout at him. "You asked me why I can't open myself up to him, that's why. You just proved my point. We're not good for each other."

"Or you'd be really good for each other, and you're afraid of getting hurt," Xavier says with his face scrunched together as he shakes his head emphatically.

"I guess we'll never know, will we? Because no matter how good you think he is for me, that doesn't change the fact that we work together, and I need this job more than I need Gabe," I say as I lean back on my chair and cross my arms like a moody teenager.

Xavier runs his hand through his hair. "You're impossible, Harper Atwood."

"Yes, Xavier, I am, but you love me and all my crazy ways," I joke. Walking inside, I look back at him and ask, "Are you staying or going? Because I'm going inside to throw up and sleep off this buzz."

Chapter 14

GABE

I take an extra long time getting out of the car and pulling myself together because the last thing I need right now is to run into Harper in the elevator or hallway.

I throw my head between my hands in the driver's seat. What just happened? How did I let this happen? We just started to get along, and now she will be cold and make things weird. She's going to make my life a living hell at work again. As much as I try to push the thought from my head, I keep thinking she may never give me another chance. It's all so wrong. Why does this girl invade my head?

"*Fuck*," I yell into my hands.

I ended things with Joy weeks ago and probably shouldn't be here, but I am, and I need someone to talk to.

Why am I worried about talking to Joy? We agreed that she wouldn't be mad. I already told her what was going on, but today makes things real. I know she'll be hurt.

I'm at a loss for words. The four black and tan drinks have caught up with me, and I can't understand my thoughts. I get out of my car and do my best to fix my shirt and hair in the reflection in my car window. The elevator ride to Joy's has never felt so long. I stand at the end of the hall that Harper and Joy share and drop my head. How can the only two girls in my life live a few doors from each other? I run my hands through my hair, take a deep, steadying breath, and knock on Joy's door. I feel like such an asshole for being here.

"Hey, Sunshine," I say when she opens the door with her usual smiling face and chipper demeanor. Not a hint of frustration about how late it is and that I'm unexpectedly showing up at her door. "Sorry, I needed someone to talk to. I also need to shower so I can sober up a bit. Do you mind?"

"Of course not. You know you don't have to ask," she says as she steps back and opens the door for me to enter.

She stops me in the living room, gives me a sympathetic smile, and says, "I'm going to finish putting my laundry away. Sit on the balcony and get some fresh air. I'll be out in a few, and we can talk."

Before I shower, I sit on Joy's deck. Sitting in the dark of the night is one of my favorite things. There's no one to hide from in the black. No one knows you. No one cares. I feel faceless out here and, in a job where I always have to be on all the time, this peace is nice.

My mind is racing a mile a minute, and a million things are plaguing me. I feel sick and have to fight to push down the bile I can feel traveling up my esophagus.

I hear a very familiar giggle and a playful slap in the silence. Instantly, I know Karma just sent me another *fuck you*.

A few balconies over, the girl I wanted to fuck no more than an hour ago is giggling with a guy. I can't see her through the pitch-black. I feel my face flush, and jealousy runs through my veins. I find myself straining to see her shadow. I need to know who she's with. Is he the reason she said no to me?

There's no moon tonight, which is making it damn near impossible for me to see them. Shadows and outlines are all the moon will allow me at this moment.

I try to look away, but her pull on me is too strong—jealousy continuing to course through my body. Reality hits me like a ton of bricks. *Go inside*, I try to rationalize with myself, but I'm glued to where I am, and I can't stop listening to her.

My cock becomes harder and harder. The pressure of it pushing against my jeans is too much. I unzip them to free my begging dick. I can still hear her. Her voice is muffled. I strain to listen to her, and I fist my cock and rub it up and down. I wipe the pre-cum with my thumb and use it as lube, stroking myself from base to tip just like I wanted her to do in my car tonight. All I can think about is her as I continue to stroke myself. All I can hear is her voice. The scent of her perfume fills the night air. When I listen to her laugh, I want to be the one making her laugh. I want to hear my name come from her lips. The sound of her voice and the fantasy of my cock in her mouth is enough to make me explode in my free hand.

Winded and out of breath, I quickly look around for anywhere to dispose of the cum I just shot into my palm.

I hear Harper say, "I have to go to bed. Are you staying or going?" On cue, I sneak inside to wash my hands and shower.

My shower is hot and long. I'm trying to push aside thoughts of Harper and my buzz so I can have a grown-up talk with Joy without upsetting her.

I dry off after my shower, wrap a towel around me, and find some sweats I left here a while ago. I scour through Joy's closet and find one of the many hoodies she's stolen from my apartment. I sit on the side of Joy's bed, pull her onto the bed next to me, and lay my head on her lap.

"What's wrong?" She giggles as she pets me like a cat. There is no anger on her face, just understanding.

"The girl from work," I say as I sit up to look at her.

"Okay, tell me what happened since last we talked," she says, still amused at my agony.

"The girl I was telling you about, I can't stop thinking about her. One minute, she's friendly. The next, she's a monster," I say, looking at her. "Joy, I'm sorry. I shouldn't even be talking to you about this."

Joy laughs again. "Gabe, we agreed to be friends. We both knew whatever this was wasn't forever." She motions between us. "If I'm being honest, I was using you to avoid having to date and worry about a commitment. Not that I don't want one, because I do. But I'm either too much or not enough for other guys, and with you, it was easy. You were my excuse not to get hurt." There is so much sadness in her voice.

"Joy, you're amazing." I shift her body to face me and take her hands in mine. "Some guy will give you his whole heart, and I can't wait to cheer you on the journey." She softly kisses my cheek.

"Can I ask you a question?" she asks as she shimmies back onto her mattress and crosses her legs.

Feeling much more relaxed than I was five minutes ago. "Anything." I answer.

"Is it the mean girl from the elevator? Because when you two made eye contact, I felt the earth shift off its axis a bit."

"Yes, it's Harper," I answer in defeat. "But nothing is happening except her taking up all the space in my mind."

"What part has you all tied up in your head, the friendly Harper or the monster Harper?"

"Honestly, Joy, we've had maybe two real conversations since we were first introduced. Any other interaction is a game of cat and mouse. The day she came in to do her pre-employment paperwork was so easy. I felt like I could spend forever talking to her. We just clicked. Then, she pulled back her veil tonight, and we laughed and talked. She's hot and cold. One minute, she's friendly, and the next, she treats me like a stranger." Then I add because it's true, "Don't get me wrong, Joy, pissing off monster Harper is a lot of fun too."

We laugh.

"It doesn't hurt that she's beautiful either," Joy adds.

"Yeah, but I'm not sure she even realizes how beautiful she is, so that makes her even more attractive."

"I get it," Joy says, nodding in agreement. "So, what's your plan to win her over?"

Shamelessly, I say, "Make her fall so in love with me. Nothing else matters."

Joy pushes me back onto her bed so I'm lying flat, and her body follows mine. We both stare at her ceiling, and she says, "Hey, Gabe, your plan isn't a plan at all, but it's a goal. You're going to need a plan to get a girl like her."

"Should I play hard to get?"

"Maybe as a last resort, but I'm not counting it out as an option for you. Maybe a girl like Harper needs a challenge," Joy assures me.

Chapter 15

I feel a hand grab my arm and pull me back as I walk down the hallway at work. I turn back to see who it is, and the electricity pulsing through my body tells me it's Gabe. I can smell his cologne and immediately feel a mix of emotions.

When we make eye contact, he says in a quiet but possessive tone, "We need to talk about last night, Harper."

Again, that ache in my chest when he says my name. We're so close our chests are almost touching. The hallway at work is small. You have to wait for someone to pass coming from the opposite direction. There's not a lot of space, and it seems even smaller when the two of us are there simultaneously.

"Gabe, there's nothing to talk about," I say with a hitch.

Not releasing my arm, he says, "I'm not letting you leave this hallway until we talk about last night."

He doesn't break eye contact with me as he moves closer into my space. His eyes are hungry but still hold enough mystery to throw me off my game. They're so dark, darker than a starless midnight sky.

I've never seen him this determined. This isn't the happy-go-lucky Gabe. This Gabe is hellbent on getting his way right now, and as much as I hate to admit it, it's hot.

I take a deep, calming breath and lower my voice almost to a whisper, "Gabe, we got too close last night after drinking too much. Just let it go."

I feel like we're sharing the same oxygen at this point.

He moves back a little, which catches me off guard. "Wait, that's it? We got a little too close last night repeats as he moves back in, closer than before. Our chests are touching now, and he adds in a husky voice, "Harper, we didn't get close enough last night. And if you think it all ends there, you're wrong. You see, I get what I want, and I want this, and I think you want it, too."

And, oh my God. This man is putting my self-control to the test. I am simultaneously managing the war between my lady parts and my brain, all while praying that no one walks down this hallway and catches us here, body to body. What am I even doing?

I do my best to sound confident and not melt against his body, which might be the only thing keeping me upright.

I tilt my head, "Don't be a child, Gabe. Nothing happened, and nothing is going to happen between us." I look down at his hand, still gripping my arm, and say, "Can I have my arm back?" even though a very large part of me doesn't want him to let go.

I want him to hold me tighter and take me right here in the hallway at work. I picture my legs wrapped around him with my skirt pushed up to my thighs. *Stop it, Harper,* I silently scold myself.

I quickly erase that image and say, "I have a lot of work to do. And don't worry about last night. Two friends had too much to drink. It happens all the time. It was no big deal," I say as I try to shrug it off.

He steps back again, but he releases my arm this time, and

I suddenly feel cold. I don't particularly appreciate that my body reacts to him the way it does.

Before he walks away, he lowers himself just a tiny bit to whisper in my ear, "Harper, this isn't over. Let me know when you're willing to admit you want me too."

I practically run back to my desk, completely ignoring the task I initially wanted to accomplish before I was accosted by demanding Gabe in the hallway. I rush past Landon.

He tries to stop me, but I hold my hand up as I quickly pass him and yell back, "Sorry, can't talk girl on a mission."

I know my cheeks are flushed, and I look deranged, but this is what Gabe does to me. He used to worm his way under my skin to irritate me, and now he's making me all hot and bothered. *I just can't with him.*

Twenty minutes later feels like twenty hours later. I can't stop thinking about Gabe. He makes me feel out of control. I lose sight of my goals when he talks to me. I don't want to be in a relationship, but all I think about is what it would be like to be with him. I didn't even want to be his friend, and now look at me when he says my name. My mind and body go to war with each other.

I need air. My mind is racing, making it impossible to concentrate on work. I look down at my desk and put my head in my hands. I have salespeople asking me questions, and I'm having a mental breakdown. I have to get air before my head explodes. I grab my purse and stop at the reception desk. "I'm going to grab a coffee and fresh air. I'll be back in fifteen minutes if anyone needs me."

"I'll tell Gabe when he comes over to look for you," she says with a sly, all-knowing smile.

I dismissively wave my hand, then quickly exit through the side door before anybody notices me leaving.

"Harper!" I hear my name being shouted across the lot.

"Fuck," I mutter, pretending I can't hear Gabe bellowing at me.

"Wait up. I'm coming with you."

He catches up to me in under seven seconds. He grabs my arm for the second time today and holds me in place as he leans forward, trying to catch his breath.

"Cardio isn't your friend?" I joke.

Still panting, he releases me and says, "You didn't think I'd let you walk for coffee alone, did you?"

"A girl can dream, Gabe," I deadpan.

"Even though I'm ninety-nine percent sure if someone kidnapped you, they'd immediately bring you back, I couldn't live with myself if something happened to you," he says as he shoves me off the sidewalk into the street, only to pull me back up onto the curb.

Our bodies collide, but he holds me against him to steady me. I can feel his pecs rise and fall with every breath, and his hands are so strong, holding me against him.

Instinctively, we stop walking. I get lost in his gaze, and every one of my muscles softens into his hold. We are so close I can feel his breath on my lips. I swallow, and I know he can hear it. His lips are pursed centimeters away from mine. My phone rings, snapping me out of this alternate universe where I was going to let the guy I've been pushing away for months kiss me. I fumble it as I try to answer it and drop it in the process.

"*Fuck!*" I shout. Pushing myself out of his hold to grab it off the ground.

"Is it cracked?" he asks as I wipe the dirt off of it onto my skirt.

Inspecting it, I shrug and shake my head no.

"I really need to get back," I insist.

"Of course you do, Harper," he says with an irritated sigh.

Chapter 16

Months have passed, and things are almost normal around the office, and when I say normal, I mean super fucking awkward. Gabe and I are so gauche when we interact. It's like two middle school kids on the playground playing chase. Gabe hasn't invited me to weekly drinks with everyone. Usually, I wouldn't care since I'd rather set myself on fire before attending never-ending social events, but I do care, and I hate that I care.

I care that he doesn't want me there, and that's scary. I have always kept everyone at arm's length, but it's different with Gabe. I can't explain it; it's just a feeling. His subtle glances, the way he walks just a little too close to me in the hallway, and what it does to my body. It's like he's trying to get under my skin or break me down. He's maddening and sweet at the same time.

All the instability with Gabe at work makes me so thankful I have Xavier. He is a fantastic listener and has nothing better to do than distract me. He sleeps over on the weekends and gives me my space on weekdays. He gets me without judgment because he knows the dysfunction I was raised in and everything I had to overcome to get where I am. I'm going to be devastated when he gets a girlfriend. I'll lose my only single friend. Julie is in a relationship, so dropping in on her is not an option.

I see Gabe's friend with benefits, Joy, at the pool and the lobby often. I'm friendly but short. The last thing I need is for her to try to befriend me. Xavier sees her often around as well, but he engages with her. I can tell he likes her, which irritates the fuck out of me. If there's one person he is not allowed to hang out with, it's her. He says she's a bundle of sunshine, and that's enough to fuel my dislike for her. He thinks it's funny, so he'll do and say things to get a rise out of me.

Xavier – I just saw your boyfriend's ex-girlfriend in the lobby, and we talked for five minutes.

Me – You're a child. I can't text; walking into a meeting, they're announcing the December sales contest. xx

During the holiday season, dealerships run several contests simultaneously. They have one for the sales guys, one for fleet, one for service, and one for the managers. We always have a hand in each of them, so our prize is always much more lucrative. Cash and tickets to some events the auto group has season tickets to. This year, it's $500 and a ticket to tonight's Sharks game for the top two sales managers. The Sharks are Los Angeles's professional basketball team. They are the best in the league and, apparently, a very hard ticket to come by.

I overheard the guys bitching about the possibly of me winning the other Sharks ticket because it could cause issues for them at home with their wives. And, of course, the obvious—I'm not fun. I'll be one of the winners. I've won every sales contest since I started. I'm just hoping Gabe isn't the other winner. I was trying to help Mark and his team increase sales so he would win with me. I haven't decided whether to attend the game tonight, but I could use the $500 cash prize.

"I knew we'd win," I say as my entire team is chanting, "Speech, speech, speech."

I don't particularly like how my voice sounds on microphones, and I have no idea what to say, so I hold up my envelope of cash and Sharks tickets and tell my team to come up and collect their winnings.

But for good measure, I shout as I hand out cash to my team, "If anyone wants to be part of the winning team, we're always hiring in E-commerce."

Shouting erupts in the room, and I watch crumpled-up paper starting to be thrown at my team. It's all done in fun. Dealerships are always cut-throat. It's a dirty business, but it's always fun when a big contest ends and the winners get to collect their prizes.

Saying bye to everyone and promising my team to make a scene on the jumbotron, I head to my car only to see Gabe waiting for me. He's leaning on my driver's door, his arms crossed, sleeves rolled up under his elbows, allowing his tattoo to be fully displayed. My car has never looked so good, and I can't help the noticeable inhale I'm forced to take as I approach him.

"I'm driving. We'll get your car later," he says.

"I'm sorry, did I miss something? You're driving?" I ask, perplexed.

"The Sharks game. I'll drive."

With a drawn-out chuckle and eye roll, I say, "The game. Of course, you won the other ticket!" I say as if we both didn't know he would win the other ticket.

Everyone knew we would be the top two sales managers. Even with my help, Mark couldn't touch Gabe's sales.

"Gabe, I'm not going to the game. I just didn't want to tell anyone that."

"Why not? Have you ever been to a basketball game?"

"When my brother played as a kid."

He laughs. "No, seriously."

"I am being serious," I say.

"I'm not taking no for an answer, Harper. Besides, I owe you."

Knowing exactly where this is going, I roll my eyes and ask, "You owe me for what?"

He shrugs. "I don't know, but I'm assuming I've done something to piss you off the past week that I need to make up for."

"Gabe, nobody in this world irritates me quite like you. Do you honestly think I lie in bed at night and play all our interactions over in my head?" He just looks at me, and I continue, "No, Gabe, I don't."

I'm so close now I can see the dimple on his left cheek as his jaw twitches. I don't think he even realizes how obvious it is. I look into his bottomless brown eyes and whisper in his ear just as I gently push my leg between his. I can feel him grow hard, and as wrong as it is, it makes me feel a little better knowing he wants to fuck me as badly as I want to fuck him.

My brain and body are at war against each other right now. I'm playing with fire. Everything I'm doing right now goes against all the goals I have for myself. If I could have sex with Gabe and never see or talk to him again, I'd throw him in the back of my car, but that is not an option for us. I see him almost every day at work, and I can't mix work and this thing between us. I pull away from him, fighting against my body and everything it wants.

He tries to say something, but I put my index finger over his lips to shush him and say, "Gabe, stop talking. Nothing you say right now will change what's happening between us, and that is nothing. Whatever happened after the bar that night, and on the sidewalk the other day, can't happen again. Gabe, we are different people."

I motion between us. "This is a disaster waiting to happen Gabe, and we work together."

Before I can get into my car to leave, he grabs my arm and shoves me into his passenger seat.

"Ouch," I murmur as I rub my arm. "What was that for?" I demand, knowing I did this to myself. I can't help it with him.

As he gets into the car, he says, "We're going to the game together."

We drive in silence until we're on the freeway. I lean over and turn on the radio.

"You don't do so well in the quiet?" he asks with a flippant tone.

I feel like I'm at an impasse here. I can take the high road and show him a little bit of who I am or continue to freeze him out. Both take an extortionary amount of energy.

"No, I can hear my negative self-talk too well in silence."

He looks at me, not saying anything for a minute, and then asks, "Are you being overdramatic?"

I shrug and say, "Gabe, I'm always overdramatic. Just ask my mom."

He asks, "Who exactly are you, Harper Atwood? We have an hour's drive ahead of us. We can sit in silence, or we can talk. I've taken you to lunch, and you fed me some top-line bullshit facts that I could get off any of your social media profiles."

"I don't have social media," I tell him.

"Who doesn't have social media?" he asks, shocked.

"I don't," I answer.

There's no reason for me to have social media. I think it's a waste of time. The time other people spend on social media, I spend on perfecting my craft by reading books. I don't think social media is good for one's self-esteem, either. If I had social media, I'd spend my time comparing what others have that I don't. I feel like it's toxic.

Gabe gives me the side-eye. "Help me dissect the evil girl behind your cryptic green eyes."

"Evil." I give him a small smile and waggle my head. "What you see is who I am." Opening my arms as if I'm presenting myself to the world, I say, "I'm just Harper. I tell people how I feel, or I don't. I live alone because I like to be alone. I—" My eyes burn, "—don't trust anyone except maybe three people. I don't think I've ever really loved anyone outside of my family and my best friend."

"But you've been married. Who could survive living under the same roof as you? Wait, did you eat him?"

"Ha, ha, ha," I say with zero amusement.

"Please, please tell me more about this poor man. Did he have any idea how evil you were? Or did he make you evil? Did he hurt you? Is he responsible for the ice princess sitting next to me?"

Gabe and I have been alone before, but I don't think I've ever seen him so carefree and jovial. He is joking, and unfortunately for me, I'm the butt of his jokes, but I like this side of him, and I hate that I do.

"Enough! *Ice princess*? You're not the first person to call me that. Is that a thing now? Do girls like to be called that?" I question.

"It's only a name appropriate for you, and by the sounds of it, I'm not the only person who thinks so highly of you."

I roll my eyes and say, "We talked about this. I didn't eat him. He didn't hurt me. If you ask him, he'll say I hurt him.

I didn't mean to hurt him. I just gave up on him," I say as I unconsciously crack my knuckles. I continue, "I grew up in a house full of either drama or silence. That type of up and down takes a toll on a kid, which continued into my childhood and teenage years. I needed to leave my parent's house when I turned eighteen. So, I moved in with Liam. He was a drug addict like my dad and an alcoholic like I was. We had fun for a few years. My parents divorced a few months after I moved out, which was the best thing for both of them, but for some insane reason, I took it hard. Not for my sake, but I think for my mom. I knew with me gone and my dad gone, she'd be lonely, and selfishly, I didn't want to worry about her. Once my parents divorced, I got married, then I got sober and realized Liam was never going to be my happily ever after, so I left. "

"So you just left?" he questions.

"Yep," I say as I shrug. "I just left."

"Do you regret it?" he asks.

"I regret moving in with him when I was eighteen, I regret marrying him because that's what was expected of me, and I regret hurting him when I left. But no, I don't regret leaving him." And that's my truth summed up in one statement.

I catch him a few times looking at me out of the corner of his eye. I don't call him out because I think I like it. This side of him, which I assume is reserved for a few people in his life, makes me wonder who Gabe really is. Is it the look-at-me work, Gabe? Is it the hot neighbor, Gabe, or this Gabe, the one I only see when it's just the two of us?

"I admire you," he says just over a whisper.

"Hm?" I ask because although I could hear his voice, I couldn't hear what he said.

"I admire you," he repeats.

"Why?" I question as I play with my hands in my lap.

"Because you know what you want, and you know what you don't want. Not a lot of people are willing to do whatever it takes to be happy," he answers with true sincerity, and it again catches me off guard.

Trying to take the attention off me and what has transpired over the last several months that I'm honestly not overly proud of, I look at him, smile, and say, "Gabe, don't give me too much credit. I'm not the strong girl you think I am."

I'm still twisting my hands together on my lap as if they'll make this conversation go away. They start to sweat a little because I'm nervous about the vulnerability I just showed him. How does he do this to me?

Chapter 17

I have never been to a professional basketball game before, and I find myself more excited than I expected I would be. Am I excited about the game or being here with Gabe? I know the answer, but I'm unwilling to admit it.

Gabe returns from the concession stand with more food and beer than necessary.

He must see the surprise on my face because he blurts out, "I don't know what you like, so I got...well, everything."

I chuckle and attempt to lighten the awkwardness by saying, "I'm starving, so I'm not opposed to a few options."

We have great seats on the second level, but they're so close together. Our arms touched the entire night, and every time they did, I could feel the hair on my arms stand as electricity ran through my body. God, I hope he can't feel it, too. This tension is foreplay without any effort.

I wouldn't say I like basketball, and I've never been a Sharks fan, so Gabe spent most of the game explaining the rules and how it works. Basketball moves fast, and I appreciate that about the sport. I spent a lot of energy avoiding asking anything not basketball-related, like how do you know so much about basketball? Did you ever play sports? What is your favorite sport? I could ask questions forever, but I don't want to know the answers to them. I mean, I do, but I don't.

When the Sharks won, the entire stadium erupted in cheers. Being my first basketball game, it was a bonus that the home team won. As much as I hate to admit it, I had a great time. Gabe was so knowledgeable about the game, and he never made me feel stupid for asking questions.

"The game was fun, considering the company," I say jokingly, giving him a shove as we get to his car. He side-eyes me and shoves me into the passenger seat again.

"Not very gentlemanly of you, good sir," I joke. "That's no way to treat a lady."

"Show me a lady," he retaliates.

"Do you shove all your dates into your car like this?" I ask.

"This isn't a date, Harper. You've made that clear on multiple occasions," he retorts as he looks at me with his brown eyes. I slowly nod my head in agreement.

Since Gabe threw me into his car tonight, I didn't get a chance to change from my work clothes. A short black mini-dress was my only option for the game. I bought a t-shirt when we got to the game and tied it in the front just under my boobs so I didn't stand out like a sore thumb. My work bag was tossed into his car along with me, and I have never been more thankful for my forethought. I often stop on my way home from work to run errands, so I always have flip-flops in there.

It's late driving home, and the car is dark, so I find no reason I can't make myself comfortable by putting my feet on the dashboard and reclining the seat just a tad.

He taps his fingers on the steering wheel, and I ask, "Am I not allowed to put my feet on the dash? I took my shoes off, and my feet are clean. See?" I say as I sway my legs toward him, bent at the knees so he can see the bottoms of my feet.

He pushes them away. "Harper, I'm driving, and it's pitch black in here, and you have a skirt on."

Adjusting back into my seat and crossing my legs in front of me, I say, "You have asked me several questions about my life and who I am, but you haven't told me anything meaningful about yourself."

"What do you want to know? I have no secrets. I told you I'm the only child. My parents are still married." His voice is quiet, almost like he feels guilty saying this to me, knowing I come from a dysfunctional family.

"To each other?" I interrupt.

"Yes, to each other," he answers and laughs.

"That's amazing," I say. "I don't think I know any parents who are still married to each other."

"Don't you believe in love?" he asks.

"Sure, I do," I answer honestly. "I'm not sure I've ever seen it, and I know I've never experienced it personally. But I'm sure the multi-million dollar romance book and movie industry isn't a made-up concept. I think everyone wants to believe in love."

"Then why are you so closed off?" he asks.

"Closed off to whom, You?"

"Yes, to me, but not only me. I've never really seen you have a conversation with anyone that doesn't specifically involve work."

"I don't know, maybe because I feel like you're a different person in private than you are at work. And I never know which is the real you. And as far as everyone else goes, I don't want friends. I didn't even want to befriend you. You just made it impossible to say no."

"Aren't you, though?" he asks.

"Aren't I what?"

"Aren't you a different person at work than in private?"

"Well, when you put it that way, Yes, I guess I am."

"So, are you saying I shouldn't trust you?" he asks.

"Yes, I'm saying that. You should not trust me one bit," I answer with all honesty. I add, "You and I share a few similar personality traits, and I don't like myself, so I sure as hell don't like them in you."

"I like me," he says.

"Trust me, Gabe, everyone who meets you immediately knows how much you like yourself," I say with a chuckle.

It's then I feel his thumb on the outside of my thigh, trailing it from the hem of my skirt to my knee. This continues for a few minutes until he wraps his entire hand around my thigh.

"What are you doing, Gabe?" My voice hitches, and it's breathy. I know damn well what he's doing. Just ask my body; it'll tell you.

"Taking what is mine," he says, and a chill forms over my entire body.

"Taking what is yours?" I nervously ask. My body is on fire right now. I need to roll down the window, but I don't.

"Taking what *should* be mine," he corrects.

I hold on to his hand to stop him from reaching my already-soaked panties. "Gabe, I need to tell you this before we go any further. I will not stop you right now. I will not feel guilty tomorrow when I see you at work. I will not look away in shame when you brush against me in the hallway. I can't even say this will happen a second time, or I'll be nice to you moving forward. So, before I let your hand go, please think long and hard about your next move because I assure you, it will change everything for us moving forward."

Pain and pleasure rip through my body when he grasps my thigh even harder. That grasp tells me more in one second than he could tell me with a hundred words.

All inhibition is thrown to the wind. I uncross my legs and

rest one between his, allowing him free range of my throbbing clit. He moves in with two fingers, not wasting any time. I whimper as his fingers enter me, and he can't stop a moan from escaping his lips. I take his right hand in mine and do my best to make him look at me even though he's trying to concentrate on driving. I slide his fingers in my mouth to taste myself on him.

A low, drawn-out mummer rumbles in his chest, and a barely audible, "Fuck, Harper, you're killing me."

I lean to him, unzip his pants and free his bulging cock. It's big in girth and length, and I find myself looking at it for a second too long before I hear him say in a smug voice, "Do you like what you see?"

I look up as he shoots me a confident smirk, showing me his damn dimple.

I answer him in the most controlled voice I can muster, "I told you I wasn't going to fuck you, so you better enjoy this moment."

"No, what you said was you wouldn't ask me to fuck you," he argues. "Eventually, I won't be driving Harper, and I won't ask either," he adds, and butterflies take over my belly.

Trying to hide my nerves, I lower myself down, leaning over the center console. I take his rock-hard dick in my hand and slowly circle the crown of it with my tongue. He lets out a throaty moan that I can feel throughout my entire body. I take just the tip in my mouth and suck as I continue to draw circles with my tongue around the crown.

He lets out another moan, and I take his entire dick in my mouth until it hits the back of my throat and I gag. Tears fill my eyes, but the sounds coming from his mouth make it so worth it. I continue to move my mouth up and down his entire shaft until I can feel him start to thrust in my mouth. His hips start moving faster and faster as the crown grows wider. I know he's close.

"Harper, you have to stop, or I'm going to cum."

I move my mouth faster and faster up and down his shaft, using my tongue to flick the tip every time I reach the top.

"Fuck I'm going to cum," he says, completely breathless. I moan, and his balls tighten, then his entire body clenches as he cums in my mouth.

With a smug smile, I quietly say, "Oh, and Gabe, one more thing."

"Yeah, anything," he says breathily.

"Don't you dare fall in love with me."

Chapter 18

I hate five a.m. alarm clocks. I slam my hand down on my phone to shut it up, throw my pillow over my head, and whine with frustration. I hate getting out of bed early. In all my years, I have never enjoyed getting out of bed. I don't understand people who get up at four a.m., work out, journal, and eat a good breakfast. My morning routine consists of a short temper tantrum, a long pep-talk to get up, a cup of coffee (or two or three), and me running out the door and speeding to work because I took way too long to get out of bed. Every New Year, I resolve to do better, and by January 2nd, I'm cursing my alarm clock.

"Shit, Shit, Shit," I curse to myself, running up the stairs to the meeting room.

It's Friday, and it's my turn to lead the sales meeting. Bursting into the door to set up my presentation, I run into a brick wall.

"Gabe!" I gasp into his chest. "What are you doing here so early? You scared me. No one is supposed to be here for forty-five minutes."

He wraps his all too strong hands around each of my biceps and pushes me away from him.

"Slow down, Harper. You're going to have a heart attack.

It's my meeting today. Did you get here to help me set up? Or did you realize you didn't get enough on the way home from the game, and maybe you missed me?"

I don't miss him, do I? I mean, I haven't stopped thinking about last night in his car, but I don't miss him. I snap out of it.

"No, no, no, no, no, no," I protest. "It's my day."

"Calm down, this is not meltdown-worthy. Just be thankful you're ready for next week."

"No, you don't understand. I got out of bed early today for this.

"And..." he says as if it's nothing.

"And I hate the mornings, Gabe," I whine. "I can't do this again next week."

He bursts out in laughter. Like real laughter. It's sweet and maddening all at once.

"Harper, are you serious right now?" he asks as he scratches at his chin.

"Yes, I'm serious. Please let me go today, and you take mine next week," I plead with him, hands together in front of my chest.

He's still laughing.

"Gaaaaabe," I draw out his name. "I'm not kidding. Please," I beg, bouncing on my toes.

"Harper, you sound like a child."

I cross my arms, stick out my lower lip, and stomp my foot. "No, I don't."

And with that, we both burst out in laughter.

He approaches me slowly, looking at me from head to toe, taking in my long black pencil skirt and black blazer. He raises a brow when he notices I opted not to wear anything under my blazer. I wasn't blessed in the breast department, so what larger-breasted woman can't get away with, I can.

Trying to escape the hold he has over me, ignore the burning in my chest, and push aside the uncomfortable feeling growing in my stomach. I say innocently, "What do you say? Can I take the presentation today?"

He moves in closer until I feel his suit jacket's lapel rest upon my bare chest. Suddenly, I miss the shirt I didn't put on this morning. I can feel his chest rise and fall against me. It's taking everything out of me not to grab his head, pull it down, and ravish his lips with mine.

I feel like I'm dying inside, or is this what living feels like? I can feel all the invisible parts of my body working. I feel my heart pumping blood to all the wrong places. I feel flutters in my stomach, and my chest feels like there's a thousand-pound weight on it. My body is waging a war against me that's impossible to ignore.

He looks down at me, and in a very controlled voice, he asks, "Are you okay, Harper?"

"Oh, um y-yeah," I stammer in a shaky voice.

Every time he says my name, I can feel my walls shattering. I can't give him the pleasure of knowing how he's affecting me, but I can't hide it either.

He drags his finger down the side of my face and brushes my hair behind my shoulder. "Are you sure? Your face is flush."

"Nope, I'm good. I'm just waiting for you to tell me if you're going to let me lead the meeting today."

Sweat is forming on my hairline, and I know he can see it.

We are so close that I can taste the tobacco in his expensive cologne, which reminds me of the first day he rescued me.

"Weeeeell," I draw out the question.

"Well, what, Harper?" he says in an almost whisper.

Why does he always have to say my name? Why does it sound so beautiful coming off his lips?

"The presentation...?"

That's the last thing I remember saying before he has my legs wrapped around his waist. He sets me on the huge conference table and stares down at me, standing between my legs, and the ache I feel in my chest is so prevalent I feel like I could drop dead of a heart attack. How can something that feels this good be so bad?

I shimmy back just a bit, but he holds me tighter and thrusts me even closer than I was before. He is there at my entrance. The only thing separating us is his perfectly tailored suit pants.

He rests me on my elbows, not taking his eyes off mine. He slowly removes his jacket, and then I hear the jingle of his belt buckle. I take a deep breath, trying not to pass out, and my eyes drift shut.

"Don't look away from me, Harper. This is my time, and I want to watch my reflection in your eyes the entire time." Another deep inhale.

His pants fall to a puddle at his ankles. Staring at me, he licks his palm, strokes his cock, then jams it into me. "Fuck Harper, you're so wet for me. You wanted me as much as I wanted you."

"I've been dreaming of this, needing this since the first night in my car. The drive home from the basketball game was just a warm-up for this." He says.

Jamming his entire length into me, I can feel his penis assault my folds. He can't get any deeper in me. He's holding me by the shoulder so I don't slide back on the conference table. The table that fifty salespeople will be sitting at in less than a half hour, and that thought brings me closer and closer to climax. He brings my head into his chest and continues to drive his cock into me relentlessly. All his pent-up tension is being unleashed on my pussy, and I can't get enough of him.

He whispers in my ear, "I heard you the other night on your balcony. I listened to your voice and imagined I was fucking you because it was supposed to be me there that night with you, Harper."

With the sound of my name rolling off his tongue, I beg, "Don't stop, don't stop, oh God, please don't stop."

The most intense orgasm I've ever experienced takes over my entire body. Wave after wave of pleasure runs through me. I fight to keep my eyes open for him, but they're so heavy, and I give in to the pleasure of seeing only darkness. Saying his name with my head falling back is enough to push him over the edge. He bites my neck and gives me one final punishing thrust before I feel him convulse inside of me.

He lets out a shaky "*fuck*."

His body collapses on mine as we lay still intertwined for only a minute. Then, his body steals a portion of my soul as he slowly retreats from our place on the table. I sit paralyzed, watching him dress himself. Suddenly, panic rushes over me, but not because our co-workers will be entering that door in a few minutes.

"You okay?" he asks. "You better fix all that." He waves his hand in a large circle, looking at me. "We'll have company in a few minutes."

Stammering around nervously, I say, "Umm yeah, I was just thinking of a way to thank you."

"Thank me?"

"Yes, for allowing me to lead today's meeting. That's what this was, right?" I say, sweeping my hands across the table.

I look at him with a sly half-smile, make my way to the front of the room, and stand my ground.

Several hours pass at work, and I've never been so thankful for a Friday. His scent lingers on me while his cum drips out of me with every step I take. I've spent the entire day trying my best to play it cool and not let the fact that I just had sex with the hottest guy I've ever met derail me. I inhale a deep breath to stabilize myself, but when I do that, all I smell is his expensive cologne.

Unable to take the anxiety rushing through me, I grab my things and try to escape out the side door without being seen. I fight the urge to break into a full sprint leaving.

I make it to my car, grab the handle, and wait for the familiar beep of my doors, allowing me access,

"Harper," he calls out from across the parking lot.

"*Fuck*," I moan. "Fuck, Fuck, Fuck why does he always catch me in the parking lot?"

I stop and turn to see him. He's standing there with his hands in his pockets, watching me.

His dark brown eyes are full of concern. He's gorgeous, standing there in the sunlight as it reflects off his dark hair. He takes a few steps closer to me, and I feel each in my chest. With each step, my anxiousness grows.

"What's wrong? Why are you freaking out?" he asks.

"Gabe, I can't do this." I motion between us.

"You can't do this now here at work, or you can't do this ever." He crosses his arms, and I see his jaw start to twitch.

"Both, Gabe, but I can't have this conversation with you at work. Just let me go before we make a scene." I get into my car and watch Gabe's horrified expression as I drive away.

Having sex with a guy is nothing new to me. Having sex with a man has never broken me down before, so why now? Why do I hear his voice echoing non-stop in my head? Why do I smell him every time the wind blows? I feel like he is splintering my soul, making me feel things I've tried so hard to bury. All my childhood insecurities are back. Gabe is too gorgeous for me; why would someone like him choose me?

I watch all the girls at work throw themselves at him, each

attempt more obvious than the one before. Everyone wants a piece of Gabe, and I can't compete with any of them. Gabe is the life of the party. He'll get bored with someone like me. I don't like to go out on Friday nights and drink with friends. I like to watch TV and drink on my couch with Xavier. Gabe has what sounds like an amazing family. Mine is everything but that. His parents won't think I'm good enough for their son. And that's it. I'm not good enough for Gabe, so this needs to end before it starts.

How does one's world implode in a matter of minutes?

Walking into my apartment, I throw my purse on the counter and flop onto my couch. The reality of what happened today comes crashing down on me. I put my wants before work. I've never had such a huge lapse in judgment. Being with Gabe today was amazing. I've never experienced sex like that. He made me feel so special, but this can never happen again.

Chapter 19

Hours later, when I arrive home for the second time today, someone is waiting for me.

I shouldn't be surprised at who is standing there, but I am. "What the fuck Gabe? It's two a.m. What are you doing here?"

He shoves past me into my apartment. "Shhhh, stop yelling."

"Where have you been all night? I've been here forever."

"Seriously, you're asking me where I've been? How about none of your fucking business," I whisper-shout at him.

"What the hell was that today? You said you couldn't talk at work, so here I am."

"Why?" I ask, confused

"Harper," He runs his hand through his hair. "I swear you never listen to me. I'm here to talk."

"It's two a.m.," I say as I look at my watch. "Have you been sitting outside my apartment all night?"

He starches his head, and I can tell he's irritated with me. "I hung out with Joy while I was waiting for you."

Jealousy takes over me, and all I see is red. "By hung-out, is that code for you fucked her?"

"Wait, what!" he exclaims. "No, I didn't fuck Joy. I told you, we're friends."

He tries to reassure me by touching my arm, but I pull away. "Friends with benefits. That's how you described her."

"You're twisting my words, Harper. Don't fucking do this right now. Don't you dare fucking push me away because you're scared."

I shrug. "I'm not scared."

"Then what is happening here? You said it wasn't a big deal. You wouldn't feel guilty. What the hell was all that, just bullshit?"

Tension builds in the room, and I feel claustrophobic. My fight-or-flight instinct threatens to take over, but he's in my house. Where the hell am I going to go? Nowhere, so I have to fight. With all my venomous words and nasty insults, I rage war on him.

"Gabe," I begin, hating the way his name tastes coming off my tongue, "Today was bullshit, the basketball game was bullshit, and any other time was bullshit. All our secret glances that everyone saw, the subtle brushing against me, your peace offerings. All bullshit. This was just a game to me. Don't you get it yet, Gabe? You have no idea who I am."

I bite the inside of my mouth as tears sting my eyes. I need him to leave now. I can't let him see how hard this is for me, and I don't know how long I can hold back my tears.

"I am so tired of hearing you telling me I don't know who you are. Who are you? *Who the fuck are you, Harper?*" He can't control his anger anymore, and sarcasm pours from his lips. "Please do tell me who this mystery girl is that we all call 'Harper Atwood.'"

"Fuck you, Gabe." A tear runs down my face, but I quickly wipe it away before he can see it.

"No, Harper, we tried that today, and you ran away like some freaked-out schoolgirl. What is your problem, Harper?

Did you or did you not feel what I felt?"

How do I answer this question? If I say yes, he'll think he owns me. If I answer No, he'll walk away, and I may lose him forever.

"No," I say, seething, "I felt nothing. You felt like every guy who came before you and every guy that'll come after you. I am begging you to get the fuck out of my apartment before either of says something we can never take back."

Tears run down my cheeks, and there is no hiding from him anymore. My words are saying one thing, but my tears are telling another.

"*Go!*" I scream.

As the tears continue to fall uncontrollably, I bury my face in my hands, my chest convulses under the weight of my arms, and I'm completely lost in sorrow. I watch Gabe walk out my door, and memories of my dad walking out our front door play in my head. Why do good memories embed themselves in your heart, but bad ones get embedded in your head and live there forever? Your heart fails you at every turn, and your head never forgets, never forgives.

Chapter 20

"Mom, it's seven a.m. on my only day sleep-in. What's so urgent this call couldn't wait until noon?" I groan into my phone.

"Breakfast is so urgent, and if we wait until noon, it'll be lunch, not breakfast, and you promised me last week we could have breakfast today."

"Mom, it's seven a.m.," I repeat my earlier sentence.

"Drink too much last night?" she asks, clearly judging me.

"No, but I was out late."

"With friends from work?" Her tone is perky and fresh.

"Ugh, no, Mother. I'll see you in thirty minutes. Can you order it for me so it's ready? I'm eating and going back to bed."

When I arrive at breakfast, my mom is sitting in a booth along the row of windows, watching people walk by as she sips her coffee.

When she sees me, she motions like she's going to stand to hug me, and I say, "Don't get up. Just drink your coffee."

"Harper, are you ever going to let people touch you?"

"I did yesterday at work, and it led to sex in the conference room and a blow-up in the parking lot, then World War Three in my apartment last night." I deadpan.

"Oh, Um, should we unpack before or after food?" she jokes.

"Seriously, Mom, I don't want to unpack this with you. I just need you to know why I'm in a shitty mood."

She bites her lip and takes a deep breath. "Who's the guy?" she asks, fearing for her life at this point but not willing to let it go.

"His name is Gabe." She motions at me like she's about to jump into a moving jump rope, and she's waiting for the perfect window. So, I reluctantly continue, "And he's the hottest guy I've ever seen, and he's funny and sweet, and everyone loves him, and the sex was amazing. Now, can we stop talking about this and eat?"

"No."

"Mother, I didn't come here to get interrogated. Do you do this to Brandon when you see him?"

"No, because he doesn't have issues like you."

I grimace. "Ew, that was mean."

"It's true," she says with an unruffled voice. "Harper, you've always been one for dramatics. You know your brother isn't. He is quiet and reserved but polite. You, on the other hand, are silent, judgmental, and mean."

I grimace even more in case she didn't see me the first time she insulted me.

She smiles and waves her hand in my direction. "See, you have a flare for dramatics. Look at your face. Harper, you've always been a loner because you're afraid people will judge you the way you judge everyone else. You're mean, so no one will try to befriend you. It's your defense mechanism. If you don't let people in, you won't get hurt. That's a terrible way to live if you can even call it living. Harper, I love Julie, but she is not enough for you. I love Xavier, but he is your cousin. He'll never replace a boyfriend."

"Ewwww, Mom," I draw out for effect.

"Don't be a child, Harper," she scolds. "Are you listening to me?"

"Along with the entire restaurant," I say with raised brows.

"Good. Please go and make some friends, if not at work, then somewhere. Go have sex with lots of guys."

"Mom!" I interrupt.

"What? You can talk about sex, but I can't?" she asks as she straightens her spine and sits up taller in her chair.

"Please make this stop," I whine into my hands.

"Seriously, Harper. You're twenty-four. Have fun, meet guys, get your heart broken, and then come back stronger. You're gorgeous, Harper. Stop telling yourself you're not. Stop making yourself unapproachable and loosen up before you're old and alone like me. Being alone is no way to live your entire adult life."

Looking down at my food, I say, "If I agree, will you allow me to eat my food before it's cold?"

Chapter 21

"Is he your reason?" Xavier asks.

I put my hand over my eyes to shade myself from the sun as I turned to face him. "Who?"

"Him," he says with a nod in the direction of the man I verbally assaulted the other night in my apartment.

Gabe walks in the gate to the pool with his beautiful sidekick in tow. She's so happy, smiling, and engaging with strangers who occupy the loungers lining the apartment pool's edge.

"Fuck," I say under my breath. "He told me they weren't together anymore."

"They're not," Xavier says. I give him a perplexed look, and he continues, "I told you Joy and I are friends. They're just hanging out. There's nothing between them. And I'll take that as a yes. He's the reason."

"Yes, what?" I ask. "Xavier, you know I can't keep up with anything you say these days."

He nods in their direction. "Gabe, he's the reason you're so mopey."

"Xavier, I'm sorry. Can we go?"

"Hell no," he says playfully. "It's just getting good around here."

I give him a playful slap on his chest. He pulls my lounger closer to him, closing the space that separated us just seconds ago. I give him a curious look, and he responds with a shrug of his shoulders. I sigh softly.

"Am I a fool?" I say quietly enough no one can hear us.

He says, "Only if you let that almost perfect man slip through your fingers, Harper Marie. I love you too much *not* to be honest. You have never looked at anyone like you look at him. Your breath is different when he's around. You stammer your speech and make a fool of yourself."

A rogue tear escapes my eyes. He takes his thump and wipes it away.

"I love you too," I sob. "But I think I fucked things up this time."

Xavier has always been there for me. He was there for me when his brother died when I should've been there for him. He's selfless. It's who he is. He was there for his mom when his dad left, and he's been there every day since Matt died.

One day, he'll find someone worthy of his love and worship her every move. "One day, when you're happily married, will you name your daughter after me? This way, I know you will think of me every day."

With a chuckle, he says, "Harper, you know you're diabolical, right?"

I shrug, close my eyes, and lay back down on my lounger.

After ignoring Gabe and Joy for as long as I can, I dive into the pool.

I feel Gabe's stare as I pull myself out of the pool. The total weight of it sits on my chest. Why does he affect me this way? I try to avert my gaze from him and Joy, but I can't. They're in the middle of the pool.

"If you know what's good for you, Gabe, you won't get my hair wet," Joy says.

"*If you know what's good for you, Gabe, you won't get my hair wet*," I say, snickering under my breath.

"Immature much?" Xavier says.

I look up with innocent eyes. "What?" I question, full of guilt.

He drops his head and chuckles. "What's your next move? Chase him on the playground? Or pass him a note in class?"

"There's no next move, Xavier. What happened between us was a mistake. A monumental mistake," I add. "I was full of regret seconds after it happened. Not only because I knew it would change things between us, but..." I trail off, and he picks without missing a beat.

"Because you're afraid you'll let him in, afraid he'll hurt you? Or because you don't believe you're allowed to be happy because you had a crappy childhood and a shitty ex-husband, so you'll do everything in your power to sabotage the only thing you've ever wanted?"

"It's done, Xavier. I said awful things to him."

"It's not too late, Harper. There's nothing heroic about living behind imaginary walls."

"I'm not interested in making things right, Xavier," I say, growing more frustrated.

"You're a liar, Harper. Who are you lying to? Me or yourself? Because you're the only one buying into it."

I attempt to avert my gaze, still discreetly watching Gabe from behind my sunglasses. The water cascades effortlessly off his sun-kissed, well-defined chest, and the sinewy strength of his arms becomes evident as he hoists himself out of the pool. He's clad in dark boardshorts that accentuate his pronounced deep V-shape and his muscular legs. His presence is captivating. His smile is irresistible and gorgeous. It makes me question if I'll ever be able to break free from the hold he clearly has on me.

Chapter 22

A few weeks have passed since Gabe and I had our blow-up in my apartment, but it feels like an eternity. Gabe avoids me at all costs lately, and when he's forced to be in the same room as me, he's cold and all business. Which I can't really blame him for since I'm the one who told him to go and told him he meant nothing and...and...and.

Maybe my mom and Xavier are right. Maybe I need to apologize to Gabe, and then I can go with the flow for once and see what happens. Have some fun and take some chances.

Gabe is in the breakroom, his back facing the door. He is engrossed in his phone as he casually types away. I decided before coming up here that I was going to take the same approach with him as he did with me.

Make myself so irresistible that he can't say no. Using one of his signature moves that he used on me, I approach him as quietly as I can, come up from behind him, and casually sit on the table, legs stretched out in front of me.

"I come in peace," I say, using one of his one-liners from when I started working here. But he doesn't bother to look up from his phone. I look down only to see he's playing a stupid game. "Can I buy you lunch? I owe you."

He looks up from his game, giving me only a split second of attention. "No, I'm not hungry."

"Neither was I when you wouldn't stop hounding me, but I gave in."

His eyes are cold as arctic ice, showing no warmth or emotion, filling the room with an unsettling chill when he says, "And look where that got us."

"Gabe, you can tell me no a thousand times, and I'll continue to ask until you say yes. I'm not the number one salesgirl because I give up. I will wear you down sooner than later," I say with a smirk on my lips.

"Harper," he says my name, making time stand still and my body warm. But he is still refusing to look up from his phone. He's doing everything he can to evade any lingering connection.

"Yeah," I say in a hopeful whisper.

Finally looking up, he asks, "Yeah, what?"

I grin at him. "You said my name."

Eyes on fire and hate in his tone, he says, "Harper, you can ask me a million times to lunch, and I'll say no. You can ask me a thousand times to forgive you, and I'll say no. You can ask me a hundred times to fuck you again, and I'll say no. Whatever there was between us is dead. So, fuck off, Harper."

My eyes fill to the rim with tears, but I will die before I let a tear slip out and show him how much he just hurt me. "Gabe…" I say out loud but stop myself.

I can say more mean and hurtful things because no one spews insults like I can, but I already did that. I'm the one who did this. It's my fault he's hurting so bad. What else am I going to say? More insults are not going to make him forgive me. So, I casually push myself off the edge of the table and start walking out of the breakroom.

Gabe calls out to me, "Cat got your tongue? Come on, I've

never known Harper Atwood at a loss of words." I tell myself to keep walking. He's saying this to get a reaction out of me. He's hurt, he's not an asshole.

I give him one more glance over my shoulder, and his eyes finally give me a hint of what's behind them, and it's not the guy I thought I knew. So, without a word, I keep walking.

Chapter 23

The tension between Gabe and me is unbearable. It's become an invisible vise that coils around all the muscles in my chest, causing physical pain that can't be denied. Gabe is furious with me and is still not trying to hide it. I thought we could be civil to each other, but he won't let that happen. It's become his relentless mission to make me miserable while I'm here at work. Disgust spills off lips when he's forced to speak to me. Hate burns in his eyes when he's forced to look at me.

Now, when I walk into the breakroom and he's alone, he'll leave before I can say anything. If he gets to a meeting early and I'm in the room, he'll pretend he forgot something downstairs at his desk to waste time. On rare occasions, when I have to go into the manager's office, he leaves. Or, if he can't leave, he pretends I don't exist. I don't think I'll ever be able to do anything to make him forgive me for what I said to him that night.

• • •

Walking into the lobby of my apartment, I see Gabe. He must be on his way to see Joy. A surge of sadness creeps in, but instinctively yell, "Gabe, Gabe, wait up!"

He doesn't look back or slow down. He knows it's me and is not interested in anything I say, which still kills me. He keeps hitting the elevator button as if doing so will get it to our floor quicker.

We get on the elevator together, and I quickly hit the close-door button, praying no one else gets on with us. He refuses to acknowledge me.

"Gabe, I've been trying to apologize to you for a month for what I said in my apartment. Can we please talk?"

Not looking at me, he says, "Harper. Since we started talking, you've been telling me you're not the perfect girl for me. Why is it that when I finally listen to you, you're here telling me you're sorry? I don't get you."

Hearing my name has never hurt so bad. It's like a knife to my chest, leaving an ache that I feel in the depths of my soul.

My voice is shaky when I say, "I'm so sorry, Gabe?"

"You've said that, Harper. It no longer matters. I'm giving you what you want!" he exclaims, looking past me now.

"U-ummm," I stammer. I'm at a loss for words.

I feel like my legs are going to fail me, and my stomach is in knots. I'm stressed, knowing I have a short elevator ride to get everything out. Nothing I say is making sense.

He slowly raises his gaze to me, and his eyes are no longer a deep, beautiful shade of mahogany offering mystery and warmth that I've grown to love but bottomless pools so dark that you'll never know what lurks below the surface. They're offering no concession.

With veins bulging in his forearms, he whispers, "Fuck you. Just because you don't know how to love anyone doesn't mean I can't. Just leave me alone, Harper. We have nothing to talk about outside of work, *ever*."

His emphasis on the word *ever* sucks the air from my lungs.

Panic pulses through my body, and I feel my world collapsing around me simultaneously. The cracks he's been able to put in my walls over the past several months are sealing up.

"I can't," races out of my mouth. "I can't leave you alone."

"What the fuck is wrong with you, Harper?"

"I just want to talk to you. Please let me explain," I beg. "I'm sorry, Gabe, I'm so sorry I said those things to you and shut you out."

"Are you done?" he asks, and I nod

"I'm not sorry you shut me out, and I'm glad you said those things to me. You made me realize how fucked up your thinking is. Harper, nothing you say will fix this. Just go and leave me the fuck alone."

And that's it. The elevator opens, and Gabe walks out. I know he'll never forgive me, and working together will be impossible. I want to cry, but I don't. Maybe I've been preparing myself for this moment for a while now. Gabe and I were never going to end up together. We're too much alike and too different at the same time.

With that realization, I know we'll make each other's lives living hell at work. When everything went up in smoke that night in my apartment, I knew one of us had to transfer.

I ride the elevator back down to the first floor, get into my car, and drive to work.

I walk into the manager's office, and all eyes are on me. It reminds me of my first day when Gabe had no idea I would be working here and his face...I'll never forget the look on his face when he saw me. I stand there for a minute until Mark snaps me back to reality.

"Harper, you okay? You look like you saw a ghost."

"Um yeah, sorry I was...Never mind, it's not important.

Can we talk?"

"Sure, what's up?" he answers nonchalantly.

I look around and ask, "In private?"

He looks at the four other managers sitting in the office and says, "Oh yeah, sure, no problem."

We walk out of the dealership to the lot, and I say, "I'm putting in for a transfer."

He nods. "Gabe?" It's a question, but it's not a question.

"If I say no, that would be a lie, but if I say yes, that would also be a lie." I continue, "It's me. I got this E-commerce department up and running. I need to go to another one of our dealerships and do the same thing. That was always part of the plan. Did I think I'd be here for at least a year or two? Yes, but Gabe and I are oil and water. I was always going to leave, but he wasn't. It's just best if I go now."

Turning to face me, he asks, "Can I change your mind?"

I smile at him. A genuine smile, one that is reserved for Julie and Xavier.

I shake my head and say, "No, I made a few calls on my way to work. It's already done. I had to before I talked to you because I knew you'd change my mind."

He wraps me in a tight bear hug, all of his large body taking mine in, and it's not a terrible feeling. Maybe my mom is right. Perhaps I need to be more sociable and put myself out there. Maybe I am more likable than I think I am and can have more friends than just Julie and Xavier.

"Mark." My voice is muffled in his chest. "If you don't release me, people will start talking."

He laughs, and I feel it through my entire body. "Harper, I'm an old man. If Gabe couldn't make you fall in love with him, they all know there's no way in hell I can."

• • •

That following Monday, the transfer was official. I asked Mark not to say anything until I was gone. I didn't want them to make a big deal about it. I wanted to sneak away without any goodbyes. Mark, knowing more than he let on, agreed to my escape plan. Looking back, no part of me thought Gabe and I could be adults about this, and if I had any hope, he answered all my questions that day on the elevator.

Chapter 24

GABE

"What do you mean she's gone?"

Emotionless, Mark replies with a shrug, "She's gone. She transferred to another dealership."

"I don't understand, why?" I feel anxiety knocking on my chest, trying to have a seat in this conversation.

"Gabe, it's not rocket science, man. She got our E-commerce department up and running to upper management's expectations, and now she's moved on to the next one."

I'm trying my best to stay calm. Did she leave because of me? Did I push her out of here, or was this the plan the entire time?

"Was that the plan the entire time?" I ask, taking deep breaths and focusing on Mark's words, but my anxiety only intensifies as I play his words over in my mind. *Harper* is gone.

How did I let this happen? My palms are clammy, and the more I try to make this not a reality, the more it consumes me. It is like a weight pressing down on my chest, making it hard to breathe.

"According to her, it was." Mark adds, "Hey man, are you okay? You look a little flush."

Ignoring his question of concern, I ask, "Wait, what do you mean, according to her? Did you know she was leaving?"

Mark rubs his hands over his face and stares at me. Then it dawns on me that he knows more than he's letting on.

I ask again, not giving him an opportunity to answer my first question, "Come on, Mark, what are you not telling me? There's no chance in hell you're choosing her over me."

"Gabe, there's no choosing. You're here, and she's gone. There are no sides to be taken."

"Tell me everything she told you," I interrupt him, fuming now.

Mark hesitates but quickly concedes. "She said she knew she'd be bouncing from dealership to dealership, but she was supposed to spend at least a year at each one."

"She hasn't been here for a year yet," I interrupt him mid-sentence.

"Are you going to let me finish or just keep interrupting me?"

"Sorry, keep going. I'm listening," I say apologetically.

"She also said it wasn't fair to either of you," he says, waving his hand between where she used to sit and me. "To stay here and torture each other. You were here first, so she put in for her transfer earlier than expected. She asked me not to tell anyone until she was gone because she didn't want to make a big deal about her leaving."

"*That's it?*" I shout.

"That's it." Mark shrugs. "What else are you looking for? Listen, Gabe, I don't know what did or didn't happen between the two of you, and it's none of my business, but the last month she was here was rough on all of us. You two are like oil and water, and it was tough to watch you freeze her out."

"So, this is my fault now. Are you all putting this on me?" I argue.

"No, Gabe, but you did everything in your power to make it hard for her to want to stay. I know it takes two to tango, and you both need to take responsibility for whatever happened between you. It looks like she did, and now you're upset about it." He walks away and adds, "I think you need to give her space. She'll come around. I promise."

She'll come around. Harper is gone. Harper transferred early. All these statements keep playing over and over in my mind. What if she doesn't come around? What if I pushed her too far? Obviously, I pushed her too far, she's gone for fuck's sake. Do I even care that she's gone? Of course I care. I've been trying to get this pain-in-the-ass girl to fall for me for months, and with a few mean words and avoidance, she's gone, and I feel empty.

No, I feel fucking shattered. I never wanted her to leave. I just wanted her to feel a little bit of the rejection I was feeling. I never wanted to be without her, and now that she's gone, it's my fault. Seeing Harper every day and not talking to her was hard, but I at least got to see her smile from across the dealership and smell her perfume when she came into the manager's office for some stupid question or just to waste time joking around with Mark.

Not seeing Harper every day is a rare kind of torture that I wasn't prepared to endure. Am I crazy? How did this girl bury herself into my soul? I found this girl in a parking garage passed out in her car, then again the following day, completely out of control. She miraculously ends up working with me. We fuck, and she runs away. Maybe she didn't run away as much as I pushed her away, but she still gave up on us first. After what she said to me that night, there was no path for us to move forward. Still, I could have been less childish in freezing her out. I should have been more professional at work.

She was supposed to be the last girl I ever dated. She was supposed to be my forever, and now she's gone.

Chapter 25

I t's been a few months since my transfer, a few months since I forced myself to start therapy, and a few months since I last saw Gabe. He texted after I left and said he was sorry to see me go but added that maybe it was for the best. I agreed. The consistent thought of how I got here helps me move forward. The aching feeling I get in my chest when I think of Gabe reminds me that I need to allow others in. Losing people hurts, and I'm tired of repeatedly hurting myself. Gabe didn't hurt me. I didn't give him a chance to hurt me. *I* hurt me. Liam didn't hurt me, *I* did. I'm the common denominator.

A few guys at the new dealership are fun to flirt with. And, on the advice of my therapist and my amazing cousin, it stays just that, flirting. I've been better at work as well. As much as I've hated social gatherings in the past, I've tried to relax and participate when I'm free.

I'm in a good place right now. Xavier and I are besties. Julie and I hang out when she's free. They know every secret I hide, and they still love me. They've never bought into the lies I used to tell myself, and they see me for who I am.

I'm a girl bruised (but not broken) from a dysfunctional childhood who refused to let people in because I was afraid of getting hurt by others' judgment. I created a make-believe reality for myself that was completely backward. I was a girl so afraid of getting my heart broken by the love of her life that I refused to even look for someone worthy of giving my heart to. A girl who was so afraid of rejection that I refused to live to my full potential because mediocrity was easier. But that girl got left behind in therapy. This girl standing here today, getting ready for her not-so-surprise birthday party (Xavier and Julie are terrible at surprises) is an entirely different girl.

I was born in the summer, and it still manages to rain every year on my birthday. Rain or no rain this year, I'm grateful everyone cares enough to throw me a party. I used to feel birthdays were a burden on everyone except my parents. I always believed no one, but my mom cared about the day I was born.

• • •

Xavier's text reminds me that he's picking me up in an Uber.

Xavier – Here

Me – Coming down now

When I see him, I jump in the car, reach over, and hug him.

"Happy birthday," he says, releasing me and giving me the once-over.

"Thanks! Are you hiding my birthday cake from your mom?" I ask only half joking and wholly not expecting an answer.

Growing up, my aunt used to make my birthday cakes because my parents couldn't afford the fancy cakes. They were always in the shape of a rabbit. Since my birthday is in the summer, I guess my birthday makes her think of bunnies. I never asked her why she chose bunnies. Maybe this time, I will.

My *not* surprise party is at a sports bar near my work. Everyone will be there, including a few people from my old store.

"Does he know about tonight, Xavier?" I reluctantly ask.

"Him who?" Xavier replies, genuinely confused

"Don't make me say his name!"

"Your therapist would say it's progress," he jokes.

"I hate you, Xavier. Gabe wasn't invited correct."

"No, but if he was, I don't think he'd show," Xavier says with too much honesty.

"Ouch, can you remove the dagger you just shoved through my heart?"

"I ordered you a rabbit cake if it helps."

"Awww from your mom?"

"You know that's not an option, Harper," he scolds.

"You know this party and all the details are supposed to be a surprise, right?" I retort.

With a wave of his hand, I know this conversation is over.

• • •

A year ago, I don't think you could've dragged me to my surprise birthday party, but tonight was so much fun. Probably twenty-five to thirty people from the new dealership showed up. Are they friends? Yes, every one of them.

We drank too much and danced too much, and I think I saw Xavier kiss a cute girl from accounting on the dance floor. Everyone sang Happy Birthday as I hid my face in my hands and blushed like my six-year-old self.

Nothing will ever ruin the memory of tonight. It was perfect.

"I'm going to Uber home," I whisper in Xavier's ear from behind. Wrapping my arms around his neck, I kiss him on the cheek.

"Thank you, cousin. I don't know what I would do without you."

It's a short drive home, but there is still enough time for my negative talk to have an opinion about tonight. Playing over things I said or didn't say makes me doubt every interaction I experienced tonight. It's in the silence they appear. They never ask for permission or wait for an invitation. Just an unwelcomed guest that refuses to leave.

"Can you turn up the radio?" I ask my driver.

I take the stairs tonight. I'll count it as my cardio for today. I can't wait to shower, crawl into bed, and work up the energy to see my mom tomorrow. I'm sure she's disappointed I didn't spend tonight with her. I always tiptoed around our old family home, trying not to bring attention to me or my wants and needs. I never wanted to rock the boat or upset my mom more than necessary for fear of upsetting or hurting her feelings. Then, once my dad left, I felt like I needed to take care of her emotionally. She was alone, and that made me sad for her. I'm alone by choice. My mom didn't choose this ending.

Opening the door to my apartment, there's a faint orange flicker from my dinette. It's darker in my apartment than in the hallway, so my eyes fight to adjust to the sudden change.

There he sits. Brown boots, the ones he often wears, dark-washed jeans, and a black button-down shirt with his sleeve rolled up just below his elbow. I should've screamed in surprise, but I knew who it was before I could even see him. I could smell the tobacco and citrus of his expensive cologne.

My chest aches, and anticipation builds, knowing I could feel his presence before seeing him. Understanding the effect he still has on me unnerves me. Every time I see him, I feel him first, and it scares the shit out of me. No amount of therapy could ever prepare me to see Gabe in my apartment again.

"What do you need, Gabe?" I ask wearily. "It's been a long time since you showed up at my apartment in the wee hours of the morning."

"I missed you too, Harper." Pain bolts through my body with those five words.

"How did you get in here?" I ask because what do I say after that comment?

"I'm here to wish you a happy birthday."

"The party is over. You missed it," I say cautiously.

All I've wanted for the last several months is for this man to show up at my door, and now that he's here, I don't know how to feel about it.

"I wasn't invited. No thanks to your cousin. However, he did make sure I had a way in so I could see you tonight."

Yeah, he's not happy about not receiving an invite.

"I thought it was for the best. We seem to have a negative effect on each other, which brings me to why you're here. If you're here to argue, I'm not going to indulge you. I'm tired, and I want to go to bed."

He looks over to me, and sparks erupt in his big, brown eyes. He blows out the lone candle on the cupcake he brought as a peace offering and takes a few steps toward me. With his advance, I take a few steps back, and the dance begins. For every one of his steps forward, I match them retreating. He has me backed into a corner...He slowly stalks over to me. I feel like his prey, knowing he's toying with me. No part of me's scared of him. Uncertain, yes, but he doesn't scare me at all.

He smells so good. Damn, I missed his scent more than I'd like to admit. All I want to do is bury my face in his shoulder and inhale him. I get lost in my thoughts for a minute too long because we're almost touching, and I don't even realize it. Before I can push him back, he cradles me in his arms, and I'm instantly off the ground.

"Gabe!" I exclaim. "Put me down."

"You said all you wanted to do was go to bed, so that's what we're doing."

"I'm sorry, Wait! What!"

"A birthday wish for the birthday girl."

"You think sleeping with you is my birthday wish?"

"Isn't it?" He isn't asking me this right now, is he?

In my bedroom, I can see his face clearly. He's serious, almost stoic. There's a battle raging inside me. I want to ask him what is wrong. I want to ask him (again) what he's doing here while wanting not to say a word and have him take me for himself.

He can see it in my eyes, but he's battling his war. His eyes gloss, and they are dark. Too dark for me to see what he's thinking.

He sits me on my bed, and I ask, "What is it, Gabe? Why are you here? We haven't spoken in months. You're not here just to wish me a happy birthday. I'm sorry about what happened between us. I'm in a much better place now. I went to you that day to apologize. Apologize for everything I said to you. I knew I was transferring stores when I followed you into the elevator, and I didn't want you to hate me when I left. When you froze me out, I got angry. I know that makes me a hypocrite, but I'm a shitty person Gabe, and I'm sorry. I didn't mean for us to happen."

He tries to interrupt me, but I stop him. "Let me get this out while I can. My lease is up soon, and I didn't renew it. I moved to a different store to get away from the memory of us. I'm moving apartments because seeing Joy reminds me of you. I don't want to be jealous of your friendship. I want to be happy for you. You were the best thing that ever happened to me, and I screwed it up. I get it. I'm learning to live with myself. So please, Gabe, this time, let's leave each other on a positive note."

He is staring at me, showing almost no emotion, and I can feel my heart breaking with every word I say to him.

"Can I say something too?" he asks.

I inhale, and he is aware of the rise of my chest as I prepare myself for what he will say next. He pauses for a minute as if trying to rehearse what he's about to tell me. He walks over and sits on the edge of my bed with me.

"The day you entered the store to sign papers, you unknowingly forced your way into my soul. I have repeatedly tried to move forward without you, and I can't. I love you, Harper, all one million broken pieces of you. I want to spend an entire lifetime putting you back together. You have no idea that no one in this world compares to you. I have made it my life's work to convince you I am right, and maybe you'll believe me. Harper, I love you. I loved you the first day I saw you. I fell in love with you for the second time when you said my name."

A tear runs down my face.

"I fell in love with you the third time when you told me not to fall in love with you," he jokes, and my lips form a slight smile, and more tears fall.

"I broke things off with Joy before you and I pursued anything physical. Please stop running from me, Harper. Come home to me, no more wall, no more wars." Agony fills his eyes.

He draws me to him, so close our breath becomes one. The tears continue to stream down my face. He wipes each of them away until his touch breaks the dam, and his attempts are futile. I use the palms of my hands to wipe tears. I'm speechless; I've tried to speak up several times, but no words will leave my mouth, so I do all my body will allow me to do and nod in agreement.

"Yes," he whispers.

Another nod is all I can muster.

I see the relief and love in his eyes through the flood of tears still streaming down my face.

He kisses me, and it's not like before. It's soft and full of love. There is more love in that one kiss than any girl should experience in a lifetime.

I pull back to speak, and he stops me. "Let me have you right now, and we can fight tomorrow."

"I just wanted to say, I love you too."

He sucks in a breath, then stands before me and slowly pulls my blouse over my head. He lifts me from the bed to remove my pants. I opt to remove my panties, watching his expression as they hit the floor. Pleasure is what I see; all the panic and fear have subsided.

His cock is already hard in his jeans, but he's taking his time savoring every minute of what is happening between us. He reaches down and parts my slit using his index finger to feel the proof of my arousal, and it can not be denied. I am soaking wet with no panties. I can feel myself dripping down my thighs.

He lowers himself to eye level with my pussy and playfully licks it once, then twice. I jump at the pleasure, and he grabs my ass so I can't move. He tilts his head sideways to allow himself the ability to flick my clit back and forth with his tongue. At the same time, his finger slowly fucks me, with then he has two fingers in me.

"Mmmmm, you taste so good, Harper."

I'm trying so hard not to orgasm in five short minutes, but it's been so long, and he feels so good.

He stops for a second, making eye contact with me, and says, "Do not deny me an orgasm, Harper. Your orgasms belong to me now. There will never be anyone that comes after me. If you deny me, I will deny you of this."

He slides his tongue into me now and fucks me with it. Then he takes his fingers and pinches my clit. I can't hold it in any longer. I beg him not to stop.

"Say my name," he insists. "I want to hear my name when you cum on my face."

My entire body starts to quiver, and I feel the rush of pleasure hit me as I scream his name and cum in his mouth. My chest heaves, and before I catch my breath, he turns me over and places me on my hands and knees. His cock thrusts so hard into my pussy that I lean forward to ease the pain. He grabs my hair and pulls me back to him.

"Don't ever run from me, Harper, or you'll be punished like this."

Slap

I shriek as he slaps my ass. Another thrust so hard it takes my breath away, but I don't move, and he rewards me with a "Good girl."

He continues to thrust into me deeper and deeper as he lowers my head to the bed. Reaching around, he strokes my clit, bringing me to the brink of an orgasm once again. I know he's close to an orgasm as well. I can feel it in the change of his rhythm, so I move toward him, allowing him deeper into me.

"*Fuck, fuck fuck*," he moans. "Stop, Harper, or you will make me cum, and I'm not ready."

I use one of my hands to reach between my legs and cup his balls. I've pushed him to the point of no return. He hammers into me with so much intensity I feel like he can rip me in half. I feel a drip of his sweat fall onto my back, but all I can hear is his balls punishing my vagina as he takes me as his. With a moan, he spills inside of me, and at the same time, he pushes me over the edge, and I experience my second orgasm. I scream his name again, and he collapses on top of me.

Panting, breathless, and sweating, he wipes my hair from my face and says, "Happy birthday, Harper."

Chapter 26

"Let's go, we're going to be late!" he yells from the doorway. I'm dressed in a slutty wench costume, and he is dressed as a drunken pirate. Both are very fitting. It's the first Halloween we're going to celebrate as a couple. The past several months have flown by. My lease was up shortly after we reconciled on my birthday.

Gabe insisted work was miserable without seeing every day, and I seriously missed giving him shit every day, so we decided I'd move into his place so we could continue to terrorize each other daily. Mark and all the guys at work thank me daily via our inner office chat. Apparently, once I left, Gabe was impossible to work with.

Gabe has been a dream come true. All the qualities I was running from in him have made me fall more deeply in love with him every day. Kissing goodnight is therapy for me, and waking up next to him reminds me that there is strength in every new day. Having my job away from him is good for me, too, but I secretly love that we're still connected.

We continue to compete at work. We've just had to change the rules to suit different locations. We compete at home and, of course, in our fantastic bedroom. I'd be lying if I said his apartment was anything less than impressive. It is within walking distance of my favorite outdoor mall. The number of times we have walked there for dinner, drank too much, and swerved our way home is too high to count on both hands. We've spent every waking moment outside of work together.

Returning to reality, I rush out of our bedroom wearing a full face of make-up. Complete with smokey eyes, fake lashes, and blood-red lips.

"How am I going to keep everyone away from you tonight?" Gabe asks as he looks me up and down.

My costume shows more skin than it covers. Long tight skirt with a slit so high you can see my tight hip. No panties (it's against the rules), and this costume works better without them, so the argument is futile.

Gabe isn't jealous and loves to show me off. He is the most possessive man I've ever dated. My therapist says part of it stems from how we met and the fear that I'll leave at the first sign of trouble.

"I hate parties, Gabe. Why do you insist on dressing up for every holiday? Halloween, anything slutty, no panties. Christmas, Mrs. Clause, no panties. Valentine's Day, black dress, no panties. Your birthday, red dress, no panties. Oh, date night, any dress, no panties. My panties miss me, Gabe."

"They get you Monday through Friday. I get the weekends and every holiday," he says as if we're co-partnering children and not panties.

● ● ●

The party is underway when we arrive, and instantly, I'm already overwhelmed by anxiety. I clutch the crook of his elbow. It's my unspoken way of saying *leave me alone for a second, and I'll fucking murder you in your sleep.* He rests his hand on mine and silently reassures me.

A few drinks later, the music plays so loudly that I can't help but dance where I stand as I watch Gabe talk to a few of our friends a few feet away. Eyes closed, swaying back and forth, I feel someone behind me grinding on me. For a split second, I think it's Gabe, but this guy doesn't fit me like Gabe does. I turn around to handle him, and it's already too late. Gabe has one knee on my dance partner, and he's face down, lying on the floor, hands by his head in surrender. There are words exchanged, but there's nothing I can make out. I grab Gabe by the flowy collar of his costume and take him into the alley for air.

"Seriously, Gabe, why the scene? He was harmless. I could've handled it."

There's no point in conversing with him while he's mad. It's a mistake I haven't totally outgrown. Usually, I ignore him and let him come to me when he's ready, but tonight he went too far.

Expecting an exaggerated fight, he grabs my waist and pulls me so hard that I lose my balance.

"Gabe, what the hell are you doing?"

He smirks at me with lust in his eyes.

"Reminding you who you belong to. I own you, Harper Atwood. No man will ever touch you again, do you understand?"

"Yes," I insist under heated breath.

He unclips his buckle, and his pants fall around his thighs just enough to free his engorged cock. I raise one leg and rest it on his hip. Gabe licks his entire palm and strokes his cock to get it wet for me, but I don't need it. I'm already dripping for him.

"I want you to fill me with your cum," I whisper into his ear while grabbing his spit-soaked cock and rubbing it between my slit.

He moans and tries to look at his cock, rubbing back and forth between me, but I take his face and repeat what he said to me the first time we fucked. "Don't look away from me, Gabe. This is my time, and I want to watch my reflection in your eyes the entire time."

He's already driving into it with all his brute force. He's been drinking. I can taste the alcohol on his tongue. I can tell by his breathing he won't last long out here. He loves the thought of someone watching us.

He has me pushed up against the wall so hard that he no longer has to hold me upright. The weight of his body is enough. He reaches down and circles my clit, not slowing down but increasing in speed and force.

"Cum in me, Gabe," I whisper, and he explodes inside of me.

Then he lowers himself to his knee and continues to fuck me with his tongue. Seconds later, I cum in his mouth. The release is too much, and I'm sure my knees would fail if he didn't force me against the wall.

Driving home that night, it's quiet. We don't talk a lot. Gabe isn't mad about my dance partner, but there's something on his mind.

I break the silence. "You good?"

"Yeah," Gabe replies without a thought.

"Anything on your mind you want to talk about?" This will be my last attempt to talk to him about what may be on his mind. Anything more will force him to shut down, piss me off, and we'll fight.

"Let's not go home tonight," he says.

"Where do you want to go?" I entertain his offer.

"The beach. We'll get a room on the water."

"You know, in a few short hours, it'll be November. Not the time to lay or play in the Pacific Ocean. We have no clothes, Gabe. We can't show up to a resort dressed as pirates." However, the irony of that statement isn't lost on me.

Determined to proceed with his plan, we stop at the house, grab a few days' worth of clothes, and head for the beach. It's hard not to question his intentions, but I don't. I've spent my entire life questioning and full of doubt, but with him, I don't. Gabe isn't one to sugarcoat things, so when he says it's nothing and he wants to go to the beach. I take what he says at face value. I'm learning to trust him with my heart, with my soul, and most importantly, with my brain.

He fought for me even when I gave him zero reason to want to fight. I watched my dad spend so many years mind-fucking my mom. I swore I'd never let anyone do that to me. It surprisingly took very little therapy to help realize no one ever tried to. I always created false scenarios in my mind, allowing my subconscious to win over reason consistently. There's so much of my past that I carry with me that I became my own worst enemy.

I often wonder if I am the only person who lets their ghosts haunt them in the silence. Am I the only person who always has EarPods to listen to books, music, or podcasts? Anything to fill the silence. But then I remind myself that it doesn't really matter. My journey is mine, and I refuse to let anyone make me feel bad about it.

We spend the next few days kayaking in the Ocean, shopping on the boardwalk, and relaxing on the beach. Maybe Gabe just needed a break from reality, or perhaps he just needed me. I don't care what his reason is for bringing us here because I needed whatever this was as much as he did.

On our last night at the beach, Gabe chartered a boat. Not

just any boat but a private yacht. A yacht that is big enough for a full-blown wedding or retirement party. I've never been on anything so regal in my life.

The moon is bright, lighting the entire sky. I lean into Gabe, rest my head on his shoulder, and say, "My favorite part of the night sky at the beach is not necessarily the moon in the sky, but more the moon's reflection off the water."

Even though I'm not looking at Gabe, I can feel his gaze on me. He listens intently, paying attention to everything I say, almost as if there's a deeper meaning.

He looks at me, then back at the water, then back to me.

"Harper," he says to get my attention.

I take my head off his shoulder, and I look at him. There it is: why he's been so distracted the last few days and why our car rides have been filled with more thoughts than words.

Gabe is holding a small black velvet box, slowly sliding away from my side and lowering himself to one knee in front of me. He opens the box and holds out what has to be a two-carat, emerald-cut diamond. The moon no longer reflects off the water but off the diamond he is holding.

"No..no.no..." I beg, panicking. I try to pull him up off the ground by his arms. "No..no...no... Don't do that, Gabe. It's too soon. You don't know what you're doing. Let's talk about this. I think you're making a mistake."

He's still on one knee, refusing to get up, just watching me while my panic plays out before him. Staring up at me, he grins.

"What are you smiling at?" I ask. "Seriously, Gabe, get up. Let's talk about this rationally," I say, still trying to pull him up from his kneeling position.

"Says the irrational one," he jokes. "Stop."

He draws out his word, trying to calm me down. He takes my hand again and says, "Take a deep breath and swallow your panic so I can properly ask you to spend every day with me for the rest of your life." He takes my other hand in his, and now he has them both locked in his. His hands are strong and warm, and I don't miss how perfectly mine fit in his. "Harper, the day you walked into the dealership a year ago, I saw you for who you are. I saw every one of your imperfections and told myself if you ever gave me a chance, I'd love and embrace them all. I've looked into your soul and know you are home for me. I'll never know why, but I knew it had to be you. You are the reason I've been greedy with my heart. I've been saving it for you. So will you make me the happiest man in the world, trust in something bigger than yourself, and say yes?" At this moment, for the first time in my life, I'm not afraid. There is no dread of judgment, no fear of getting hurt, and no anxiety over what comes next. I am consumed by his overwhelming love for me, and for once in my life, I finally believe that I can have it all. I can have genuine love and passion without the crumpling fear of heartbreak.

With him, I finally feel like I am enough, and I know he will go to any length to ensure my happiness. His need for me, for my love, crashes over me like a tidal wave. But this time, it's not a tumultuous tide that repeatedly pulls me underwater only to tease me with the surface, only to drag me under again. It's the perfect wave that surfers patiently wait hours four. It's the ideal wave, the last one of the day, the wave you ride all the way to the shore.

With tears streaming down my face, I cup his face in my hands. "I can't think of anywhere I'd rather be than right here, right now. I want to make you happy. I want to be a better person every day for you. I want to sleep with you, wake up to you, and fight with you until we're both too old and gray to care. I love you, Gabe Jones. Yes. Yes, yes, yes, and *yes*!"

Epilogue

"Harper, babe, wake up," I hear Gabe whispering as he tries to shake me awake.

I moan and throw my pillow over my head. "No, it's early still."

"Get-up! It's Hazel's first day of high school. She's already knocking on our door. She needs you to help her with her hair. I made your coffee, and you'll need it before dealing with the monster outside the safety of our doors. She's as mean as you are when she's stressed. I have to go before I'm late for work. I think it's best if I allow the two of you to kill each other without any witnesses."

"Don't leave me alone with her. It's too early," I plead.

He kisses me goodbye and leaves me with our only daughter. She has so many of my features that people say we're twins. She is a little shorter than I was at her age, but she is anything but average. Her green eyes are warm and beautiful, whereas mine were cold and damaged at that age. Her skin is olive like mine, and her hair is darker, longer, and thicker than mine. She has the most fantastic skin, free of blemishes. Last year, she got her braces off, and she is stunning. Oh, and she has her dad's dimple. Everyone says we better be ready for when boys come calling on her, but I've been prepared since the first day I felt her move inside of me.

She wasn't planned, and we have always been more than

honest with her. I kept falling asleep at my desk at work. I was starting to think I was gravely ill. A close co-worker, Kelly, asked if I might have been pregnant. I missed a day of birth control and was on antibiotics, a known dangerous combination. But I still thought it would never happen to me. Reality set and, in pure panic, overtook me.

I ran to the drugstore to get a pregnancy test. I took it into the restrooms at work. Two pink lines. Equal parts panic and confusion overtook me as I ran to Kelly's office, waving the stick full of my pee in the air and yelling, "What does this mean?" Kelly looked closer as I shoved the stick under her nose and then straight into her line of sight.

She moved away and said, "Harper, you're flinging pee all over my office." But the good sport she is, told in the most loving voice, "It looks like you and Gabe are having a baby."

Stunned, anxious, and unable to concentrate on work, I drove to the drugstore (again). I bought a bib that said "#1 Dad." Determined to make it memorable for Gabe, I hurried home. He was in the kitchen with two friends, eating chocolate chip cookies. I love his friends and have never cared when they were at our house, but that day was different, and they were not part of my plan.

"Gabe, come in the garage with me," I impatiently asked.

I'm sure my sharp bitchy tone drew the attention of his waiting friends. Gabe, having no clue what was coming next, leisurely walked to the garage, asking, "What's up, babe?" On a typical day, any of these single actions would not have phased me, but that night, overrun with emotion and hormones, I snapped. I took my nicely wrapped surprise, shoved it in his chest, and yelled, "*Here!*"

That's it. That's all he got. Not, *we're having a baby...or you're about to be a dad.* Nope. Just "Here."

Despite all that and more, we've been married for seventeen years, and he still tells that story to any stranger willing to listen. They say having a kid changes sex and marriages, but our sex is even better than that first time in that boardroom. We have never been able to go longer than a day or two without ravishing each other. And the places we've made love are something we enjoy reliving in private when we get lost in conversation. It is hard not to get lost in nostalgia.

Now that Hazel is older, I try to teach her healthy boundaries with boys. She has had the privilege of learning how a man should treat a lady by watching her dad. He opens doors for us, buys us flowers, and gives her anything she wants. She watches him wash dishes with me and make the bed. We show her marriage is about being life partners.

I try to make her understand what happens when she gives herself to a boy. "With every sexual encounter, you change a little bit," I say on repeat. I tell her I hope she'll find a man who can't live without her. She always asks very sincerely. "How will I know"?

"Because you won't be able to live without him either. Your souls will know before you do," I tell her.

I don't know if I believe in soulmates or one person for everyone, but no other man would've healed my childhood wounds and made me whole as Gabe did. Since being with Gabe, I have accepted who my parents were, but more than that, I have accepted who they are now. In my eyes, my dad is no longer an abusive drug addict who uses women to hurt my mom but a fantastic grandpa who has spent more time with Hazel when she was little than I could've ever hoped for.

Maybe Hazel is his second chance. My mom, who allowed us to believe she was weak, was always controlling her destiny. It wasn't until I was an adult that I realized how strong she really was. She and Hazel have a fantastic relationship. They talk and text daily. Maybe Hazel is her second chance as well.

I have friends, so many friends. It wasn't easy getting there, but thanks to Xavier and his beautiful wife, who introduced me to all her friends, who then quickly became my friends, I have a large social group. We have raised our girls together and have become more than just friends; we have become family.

We have shown Hazel so much love that I couldn't imagine her settling for anything less as an adult.

What I've learned by watching my daughter grow up is:

My marriage is fantastic because I work to make it good.

My relationship with my husband is excellent because we take care of each other.

My daughter is blessed because she has us, and we have her.

My life was always mine to mold.

Acknowledgments

To my beloved husband,

Thank you for your unwavering support and endless patience. Thank you for sitting beside me for hours while I type so I'm not alone. Your unwavering encouragement, confidence, and belief in me have been my guiding light, and I am endlessly grateful for you. I couldn't have done this without you by my side. I love you, Por Vida.

To my daughter,

You are one of my greatest joys and a constant source of love and motivation. Your presence has been a reminder never to give up. I am so proud to be your parent and hope to make you proud.

To my dedicated editor, Sara,

Thank you for your invaluable feedback, tireless dedication, and unwavering commitment to bringing this story to life. Your keen eye for detail, insightful suggestions, and steadfast support have helped shape this book into something I am genuinely proud of. I am grateful for your expertise, professionalism, and passion for storytelling, and I look forward to continuing our creative collaboration.

To my talented book designer, Vanessa,
Your creativity and attention to detail have breathed life into the pages of this book. Thank you for your tireless dedication in crafting the layout. And to the cover design—you absolutely nailed it. Your vision perfectly captured the book's essence, and I couldn't be more thrilled with the result. Your work has truly made this book shine, and I am immensely grateful for your contribution to bringing my story to life.

About the Author

Kara Jefferies writes realistic Contemporary Romance novels, weaving tales with characters you can't help but fall in love with, coupled with enough family drama to keep you turning the pages. With a love for happy endings, she guides readers through the ups and downs of love, making the journey as rewarding as the destination.

When she's not lost in the world of writing, you'll find Kara chasing the sun on a beach alongside her husband. Though born and raised in Southern California, she now calls Texas home, sharing it with their three beloved dogs and teenage daughter.

An avid runner, Kara is also known for her love of coffee, sweets, and all things beauty.

Made in the USA
Columbia, SC
09 June 2024

36425445R00098